A DIGEST ON CRYPTOCURRENCY

Ansh Verma

Table of Contents

INTRODUCTION TO CRYPTO CURRENCY

Crypto currency is a revolutionary form of digital or virtual currency that operates on the principles of cryptography and blockchain technology. Unlike traditional fiat currencies issued by governments and central banks, cryptocurrencies are decentralized and not controlled by any single authority. The first and most well-known cryptocurrency is Bitcoin, created by an anonymous person or group of people using the pseudonym Satoshi Nakamoto in 2009. Since then, thousands of other cryptocurrencies, commonly known as altcoins, have emerged, each with its unique features and use cases.

At the core of cryptocurrency is the blockchain, a distributed ledger that records all transactions across a network of computers (nodes) in a secure, transparent, and immutable manner. Transactions are verified by network participants through a consensus mechanism, which ensures the integrity of the blockchain and prevents fraudulent activities.

One of the key features of cryptocurrencies is their ability to facilitate peer-to-peer transactions without the need for intermediaries like banks. This makes them more accessible and cost-effective, especially for cross-border transactions. Additionally, cryptocurrencies offer a high degree of privacy and pseudonymity for users, though the level of anonymity varies among different cryptocurrencies.

The value of cryptocurrencies is determined by market demand and supply dynamics, and their prices can be highly volatile. As a result, many individuals view cryptocurrencies as investment assets, speculating on their potential for significant returns.

The introduction of cryptocurrencies has also led to the emergence of decentralized finance (DeFi) and smart contract platforms, expanding their applications beyond simple monetary transactions. DeFi allows for the creation of various financial products and services without the need for traditional intermediaries, making financial services more inclusive and accessible to a broader population.

While cryptocurrencies have garnered significant attention and popularity, they also face challenges and controversies. Concerns related to security, regulatory compliance, environmental impact, and potential use in illicit activities have led to ongoing discussions about their long-term sustainability and mainstream adoption.

Overall, cryptocurrency represents a paradigm shift in the world of finance and technology, challenging traditional financial systems and offering new opportunities for innovation, economic empowerment, and financial inclusion. As the technology continues to evolve, it remains a subject of fascination and ongoing exploration by individuals, businesses, and policymakers around the globe.

HISTORY OF CRYPTOCURRENCY

The history of cryptocurrency dates back to the late 20th century, with significant milestones and key developments leading to the creation and widespread adoption of digital currencies. Here is an overview of the essential events in the history of cryptocurrency:

1. *Predecessors to Cryptocurrency:* The concept of digital currency can be traced back to the 1980s when cryptographers like David Chaum introduced the idea of cryptographic electronic money. Chaum's work laid the foundation for the concept of secure and private digital transactions.

2. *DigiCash:* In the early 1990s, David Chaum founded DigiCash, which became one of the first attempts at creating an anonymous digital currency. Despite innovative ideas, DigiCash faced challenges with adoption and eventually ceased operations in the late 1990s.

3. ***Bitcoin's Genesis:*** The breakthrough moment in the history of cryptocurrency came in 2009 when an unknown individual or group using the pseudonym Satoshi Nakamoto introduced Bitcoin, the first decentralized digital currency. Nakamoto's whitepaper titled "Bitcoin: A Peer-to-Peer Electronic Cash System" outlined the mechanics of a peer-to-peer electronic payment system based on blockchain technology.

4. ***Mining and Early Adoption:*** Bitcoin's creation was accompanied by the process of mining, where participants (miners) validate transactions and add them to the blockchain in exchange for newly minted bitcoins. The early days of Bitcoin saw a small but dedicated community of enthusiasts and developers embracing the new technology.

5. ***Growth of Altcoins:*** In the years following Bitcoin's launch, other cryptocurrencies, commonly referred to as altcoins, started to emerge. In 2011, Litecoin (LTC) was introduced, followed by many others, including Namecoin (NMC) and Ripple (XRP).

6. ***Market Expansion:*** By 2013, the cryptocurrency market had experienced significant growth, with Bitcoin's value surpassing $100 for the first time. The rise of

cryptocurrency exchanges, such as Mt. Gox, facilitated the buying, selling, and trading of various cryptocurrencies, contributing to their popularity.

7. ***Blockchain Beyond Currency:*** While Bitcoin remained the dominant cryptocurrency, the underlying blockchain technology gained attention for its potential applications beyond digital currency. Entrepreneurs and developers explored the use of blockchain in areas like supply chain management, healthcare, and decentralized finance (DeFi).

8. ***Ethereum and Smart Contracts:*** In 2015, Ethereum was introduced by Vitalik Buterin, offering a platform for developers to build decentralized applications (dApps) using smart contracts. Smart contracts are self-executing contracts with the terms directly written into code, enabling programmable and automated actions without intermediaries.

9. ***Initial Coin Offerings (ICOs):*** The mid-2010s saw the rise of ICOs as a fundraising mechanism for blockchain projects. Startups issued their own digital tokens to raise capital, attracting significant investment and sometimes controversy due to potential scams and lack of regulatory oversight.

10. ***Cryptocurrency Boom and Bust:*** The end of 2017 witnessed an unprecedented surge in cryptocurrency prices, with Bitcoin reaching an all-time high of nearly $20,000. However, the market experienced a sharp correction in 2018, leading to a period of volatility and regulatory scrutiny.

11. ***Institutional Interest:*** In recent years, institutional investors and major corporations have shown increasing interest in cryptocurrencies and blockchain technology. Financial institutions, including PayPal and Square, started offering cryptocurrency services, further validating their potential as a legitimate asset class.

12. ***DeFi and NFTs:*** The evolution of decentralized finance (DeFi) in the 2020s has provided a platform for various financial services and products to be offered in a decentralized and permissionless manner. Additionally, the rise of non-fungible tokens (NFTs) has created a new market for digital art, collectibles, and unique digital assets.

Overall, the history of cryptocurrency reflects a journey of innovation, challenges, and paradigm shifts in the financial and technological landscape. As the technology continues to mature, the future of cryptocurrency remains an exciting and ever-evolving realm of exploration and growth.

BLOCKCHAIN TECHNOLOGY

Blockchain technology is the foundational technology behind cryptocurrencies like Bitcoin, but its applications extend far beyond digital currencies. At its core, blockchain is a decentralized and distributed digital ledger that records transactions across multiple computers (nodes) in a secure, transparent, and immutable manner. Each transaction, referred to as a block, is cryptographically linked to the previous block, forming a chain of blocks, hence the name "blockchain."

Key characteristics of blockchain technology include:

1. *Decentralization:* Blockchain operates on a peer-to-peer network without the need for a central authority, making it resistant to single points of failure and censorship.

2. *Transparency:* All transactions on the blockchain are visible to all network participants, ensuring transparency and accountability.

3. *Immutability:* Once a block is added to the blockchain, it becomes nearly impossible to alter or delete its contents, ensuring the integrity and permanence of data.

4. *Security:* The cryptographic nature of blockchain ensures the authentication and validity of transactions, making it highly secure against fraudulent activities.

5. *Consensus Mechanisms:* To achieve agreement on the validity of transactions, blockchain networks use various consensus mechanisms, such as Proof of Work (PoW) and Proof of Stake (PoS).

Blockchain technology finds applications in various industries and use cases:

1. *Cryptocurrencies:* As the pioneering application, cryptocurrencies use blockchain to enable secure and transparent peer-to-peer transactions without the need for intermediaries.

2. *Supply Chain Management:* Blockchain can be used to track and verify the provenance of products throughout the supply chain, enhancing transparency and combating counterfeiting.

3. *Decentralized Finance (DeFi):* Blockchain underpins DeFi platforms, enabling the creation and execution of

smart contracts that automate financial services like lending, borrowing, and yield farming.

4. *Healthcare:* Blockchain can facilitate secure sharing of electronic health records, ensuring privacy and interoperability among healthcare providers.

5. *Voting Systems:* Blockchain technology can enhance the integrity of voting systems by providing an immutable and tamper-resistant ledger for recording votes.

6. *Identity Management:* Blockchain can enable self-sovereign identity solutions, allowing individuals to control and share their identity information securely.

7. *Internet of Things (IoT):* By providing a secure and decentralized infrastructure, blockchain can enhance the reliability and privacy of IoT devices and data.

Despite its immense potential, blockchain technology faces challenges, including scalability, energy consumption (in PoW-based blockchains), and regulatory considerations. As the technology continues to evolve, ongoing research and development are focusing on addressing these challenges and unlocking new possibilities for blockchain applications in various sectors, shaping the future of digital transactions and decentralized systems.

CRYPTOCURRENCY MINING

C ryptocurrency mining is a crucial process that underpins the operation and security of blockchain networks, particularly in proof-of-work (PoW) based crypto currencies like Bitcoin. Mining involves the validation of transactions and the addition of new blocks to the blockchain. Miners, who are participants in the network, compete to solve complex mathematical puzzles using computational power. The first miner to find the solution gets to add a new block to the blockchain and is rewarded with newly minted cryptocurrency, along with any transaction fees from the included transactions.

Here are key aspects of cryptocurrency mining:

1. *Validation of Transactions:* When users initiate cryptocurrency transactions, they are broadcasted to the network. Miners collect these transactions into blocks and verify their validity before including them in a new block.

2. *Proof-of-Work:* In PoW-based block chains like Bitcoin, miners must find a specific value, called a nonce, that, when combined with the data of the block and passed through a hashing algorithm, produces a hash value that meets certain criteria (e.g., starts with a specific number

of leading zeros). Finding this nonce involves substantial computational effort and is often described as "proof-of-work."

3. ***Difficulty Adjustment:*** The difficulty of the mathematical puzzles is dynamically adjusted to ensure that new blocks are added to the blockchain approximately every 10 minutes. If more miners join the network, the difficulty increases, and vice versa.

4. ***Consensus Mechanism:*** The process of mining facilitates consensus in the blockchain network. Once a block is successfully mined, other miners verify the solution, ensuring that the proposed block is legitimate. If the majority of the network agrees that the block is valid, it is added to the blockchain, and the process continues with the next block.

5. ***Mining Rewards:*** Miners are incentivized to participate in the process by receiving rewards in the form of newly minted cryptocurrency and transaction fees. The reward serves as an incentive to secure the network and ensures the continued operation of the blockchain.

6. ***Mining Pools:*** Due to the intense computational power required for mining, individual miners often join mining pools, where they combine their resources and share the

rewards proportionally to their contributions. Mining pools increase the likelihood of finding blocks but also distribute the rewards among pool members.

7. ***Energy Consumption:*** Cryptocurrency mining, especially in PoW systems, demands significant computational power, resulting in high energy consumption. This has led to discussions about the environmental impact of mining and efforts to explore more energy-efficient consensus mechanisms like proof-of-stake (PoS).

Cryptocurrency mining plays a critical role in securing the blockchain network, validating transactions, and ensuring the integrity of the distributed ledger. While it has been a fundamental part of the crypto ecosystem since its inception, mining continues to evolve, with ongoing discussions about its environmental impact and the development of alternative consensus mechanisms to address scalability and energy efficiency concerns.

POPULAR CRYPTOCURRENCIES

As the cryptocurrency market has grown, numerous cryptocurrencies have emerged, each with its unique features and use cases. Here are some of the most popular and well-known cryptocurrencies as of my last update in September 2021:

1. *Bitcoin (BTC):* Launched in 2009 by an anonymous person or group using the pseudonym Satoshi Nakamoto, Bitcoin is the first and most famous cryptocurrency. It operates on a decentralized blockchain and is often referred to as "digital gold." Bitcoin's primary use case is as a store of value and a medium of exchange, and it has gained widespread adoption and recognition as a global digital asset.

2. *Ethereum (ETH):* Created by Vitalik Buterin in 2015, Ethereum is a decentralized platform that enables the development of smart contracts and decentralized applications (dApps). It introduced the concept of programmable blockchain, allowing developers to build a wide range of applications, including DeFi protocols, NFT marketplaces, and more.

3. *Binance Coin (BNB):* Binance Coin is the native Cryptocurrencies of Binance, one of the largest

cryptocurrency exchanges globally. Initially launched as an ERC-20 token on the Ethereum blockchain, BNB later migrated to Binance's own block chain, Binance Smart Chain (BSC). BNB is used to pay for transaction fees on the Binance exchange and is also an integral part of the Binance Smart Chain ecosystem.

4. *Cardano (ADA):* Cardano is a blockchain platform that aims to provide a more secure and sustainable infrastructure for the development of smart contracts and dApps. It distinguishes itself through a research-driven approach, peer-reviewed academic papers, and a layered architecture designed to address scalability and sustainability issues.

5. *Ripple (XRP):* Ripple is both a digital payment protocol and a cryptocurrency. It is designed to enable fast and cost-effective cross-border transactions, particularly for financial institutions. Ripple's consensus algorithm, known as the XRP Ledger, helps facilitate transactions and settlement in near real-time.

6. *Solana (SOL):* Solana is a high-performance blockchain platform known for its fast transaction speeds and low fees. It is designed to support decentralized applications and DeFi projects, offering scalability and high

throughput compared to some other blockchain networks.

7. ***Polkadot (DOT):*** Polkadot is a multi-chain blockchain platform that aims to enable interoperability between different blockchains. It allows independent blockchains to communicate and share data, promoting cross-chain functionality and enhancing scalability and security.

8. ***Chainlink (LINK):*** Chainlink is an oracle network that connects smart contracts with real-world data and external systems. Oracles provide the necessary information for smart contracts to execute based on real-world events, making Chainlink an essential component in the development of decentralized applications.

9. ***Litecoin (LTC):*** Litecoin is often referred to as "digital silver" to Bitcoin's "digital gold." It was created by Charlie Lee in 2011 and is similar to Bitcoin in terms of its underlying technology. Litecoin aims to offer faster transaction confirmation times and lower fees compared to Bitcoin.

10. ***Uniswap (UNI):*** Uniswap is a decentralized exchange (DEX) built on the Ethereum blockchain. It allows users to swap various ERC-20 tokens directly from their wallets without the need for an intermediary. Uniswap's

decentralized nature and automated market-making (AMM) model have contributed to its popularity within the DeFi space.

It's important to note that the cryptocurrency market is highly dynamic and constantly evolving, with new cryptocurrencies and projects being introduced regularly. While these are some of the popular cryptocurrencies as of my last update, their rankings and status may have changed since then. It's always recommended to conduct thorough research and exercise caution when investing or using cryptocurrencies

CRYPTOCURRENCY EXCHANGES

Cryptocurrency exchanges are online platforms that facilitate the buying, selling, and trading of cryptocurrencies. They play a vital role in the cryptocurrency ecosystem by providing a marketplace where users can exchange their digital assets for other cryptocurrencies or fiat currencies like the US Dollar, Euro, or other national currencies. Cryptocurrency exchanges come in various types and can be centralized or decentralized.

Here are the main types of cryptocurrency exchanges:

1. *Centralized Exchanges (CEX):* Centralized exchanges are the most common type and operate as third-party intermediaries that facilitate trades between buyers and sellers. They maintain custody of users' funds and act as custodians of the private keys needed to access and manage the cryptocurrencies. CEXs often offer a user-friendly interface, advanced trading tools, and liquidity, making them popular among traders and investors. Some well-known centralized exchanges include Binance, Coinbase, Kraken, and Bitfinex.

2. *Decentralized Exchanges (DEX):* Decentralized exchanges operate on blockchain technology and do not rely on a central authority to hold users' funds. Instead,

trades are conducted directly between users through smart contracts, allowing for peer-to-peer transactions without the need for an intermediary. DEXs prioritize user privacy and control over their funds, as users retain ownership of their private keys. However, DEXs may have lower liquidity and may not offer as many trading options as centralized counterparts. Examples of DEXs include Uniswap, SushiSwap, and PancakeSwap.

3. *Hybrid Exchanges:* Hybrid exchanges combine elements of both centralized and decentralized exchanges. They may utilize a centralized order book for liquidity and speed while allowing users to retain control of their funds through non-custodial wallets. This hybrid model aims to balance the benefits of both CEXs and DEXs.

4. *Peer-to-Peer (P2P) Exchanges:* P2P exchanges enable direct trades between buyers and sellers without the involvement of a centralized platform. Users interact with each other and negotiate terms, such as price and payment method, before executing the trade. P2P exchanges are popular in regions with limited access to traditional banking services and strict cryptocurrency regulations.

5. *Fiat-to-Crypto Exchanges:* Fiat-to-crypto exchanges allow users to purchase cryptocurrencies using fiat currencies like USD, EUR, or others. These exchanges often require users to complete a verification process, known as Know Your Customer (KYC), to comply with regulatory requirements.

6. *Crypto-to-Crypto Exchanges:* Crypto-to-crypto exchanges enable users to trade one cryptocurrency for another. They offer a wide variety of trading pairs, allowing users to exchange their holdings for different cryptocurrencies based on market demand and preference.

Choosing the right cryptocurrency exchange depends on factors such as security, fees, available trading pairs, user interface, customer support, and regulatory compliance. It's essential for users to conduct thorough research and consider their specific needs and priorities before selecting an exchange to ensure a safe and satisfactory trading experience.

CRYPTO WALLETS

Cryptocurrency wallets are digital tools that allow users to store, manage, and interact with their cryptocurrencies securely. Unlike traditional wallets, cryptocurrency wallets do not hold physical currency but store the private keys necessary to access and manage the user's digital assets on the blockchain. These wallets come in various types, each offering a different level of security and ease of use.

Here are the main types of cryptocurrency wallets:

1. *Software Wallets:* a. Desktop Wallets: Desktop wallets are software applications installed on a user's computer. They provide full control over the private keys and offer a secure way to store cryptocurrencies. Popular desktop wallets include Electrum (Bitcoin), Exodus, and Atomic Wallet.

2. *Mobile Wallets:* Mobile wallets are applications designed for smartphones and tablets. They are convenient and portable, making them suitable for everyday transactions. Some mobile wallets offer

features like QR code scanning and Near Field Communication (NFC) for easy payments. Examples of mobile wallets are Trust Wallet, Coinbase Wallet, and Mycelium.

3. *Web Wallets:* Web wallets, also known as online wallets, operate through web browsers. They allow users to access their cryptocurrencies from any internet-connected device. Web wallets are convenient but come with the caveat that they are managed by a third-party service, which means users do not have full control over their private keys. Some popular web wallets include MetaMask, MyEtherWallet (MEW), and Binance Web Wallet.

4. *Hardware Wallets:* Hardware wallets are physical devices designed specifically to store cryptocurrencies securely offline. They are considered one of the most secure options because private keys are stored on the device and never exposed to the internet. Hardware wallets are often protected with a PIN or passphrase, adding an extra layer of security. Popular hardware wallets include Ledger Nano S, Ledger Nano X, Trezor, and KeepKey.

5. ***Paper Wallets:*** Paper wallets involve generating a physical copy of a user's private and public keys on paper. They are completely offline and, therefore, immune to online threats. Users can generate paper wallets using various online tools and print them for safekeeping. However, it's crucial to ensure the security of the printing process and protect the paper wallet from physical damage.

6. ***Brain Wallets:*** Brain wallets rely on memorized passphrases or mnemonics to access and recover cryptocurrencies. Users create their private keys based on a phrase or sequence of words, making it essential to choose a complex and unique passphrase. Brain wallets can be risky, as forgetting or losing the passphrase can result in permanent loss of funds.

It's crucial to practice proper security measures regardless of the type of cryptocurrency wallet used. This includes enabling two-factor authentication (2FA), keeping software and firmware up to date, regularly backing up private keys, and being cautious of phishing attempts. Users should also consider the amount of cryptocurrency they intend to store in each wallet and choose the one that aligns with their security needs and risk tolerance.

CRYPTOCURRENCY INVESTMENT AND TRADING

Cryptocurrency investment and trading have become increasingly popular as the crypto market continues to grow and evolve. However, it's important to understand that investing and trading in cryptocurrencies come with risks, and individuals should exercise caution and conduct thorough research before getting involved. Here are some key aspects of cryptocurrency investment and trading:

1. Investment vs. Trading:

- *Investment:* Cryptocurrency investment involves buying and holding digital assets for the long term with the expectation that their value will increase over time. Investors often take a "buy and hold" approach, focusing on the potential long-term growth and utility of the cryptocurrencies they choose to invest in.

- Trading: Cryptocurrency trading involves buying and selling digital assets with the aim of making short-term profits from price fluctuations. Traders use various strategies, such as technical analysis and market trends, to make informed decisions on when to enter or exit positions.

2. *Risk Management:*

   - Cryptocurrency investment and trading carry inherent risks due to the market's high volatility. It's essential to establish a risk management strategy, including setting stop-loss orders and managing position sizes, to protect capital and minimize potential losses.

3. *Due Diligence:*

   - Before investing in any cryptocurrency, conduct thorough research on the project's fundamentals, team, technology, use case, and community support. Look for credible sources of information and stay informed about industry news and developments.

4. *Diversification:*

- Diversifying a cryptocurrency portfolio can help mitigate risk. Instead of investing solely in one cryptocurrency, spread investments across multiple projects and asset classes to reduce exposure to individual asset risks.

5. **Wallet Security:**

   - Ensure the security of cryptocurrency holdings by using secure wallets, such as hardware wallets or software wallets with strong encryption. Avoid keeping large amounts of cryptocurrency on exchange wallets, as they are susceptible to hacking.

6. **Market Analysis:**

   - For traders, understanding market trends and conducting technical analysis can aid in making informed decisions. Various tools and indicators are available to help identify potential entry and exit points for trades.

7. **Emotional Discipline:**

   - Emotions can influence investment and trading decisions. Successful investors and traders maintain emotional discipline, avoiding impulsive actions based on fear or greed.

8. *Regulatory Compliance:*

- Be aware of the regulatory landscape surrounding cryptocurrencies in your country. Compliance with tax regulations and any reporting requirements is crucial for legal and financial purposes.

9. *Keep Learning:*

- The cryptocurrency market is constantly evolving, and staying updated with the latest trends, technology advancements, and market news can provide valuable insights for making informed decisions.

Cryptocurrency investment and trading can offer opportunities for financial growth and diversification, but they also involve risk. Individuals should consider their risk tolerance, investment goals, and level of knowledge before participating in the crypto market. Consulting with financial advisors or experts in the cryptocurrency space can also be beneficial for newcomers seeking guidance.

DECENTRALIZED FINANCE (DEFI)

Decentralized Finance, often referred to as DeFi, is a rapidly growing movement in the cryptocurrency space that aims to recreate traditional financial services and products on blockchain networks in a decentralized and permissionless manner. DeFi projects leverage smart contracts, which are self-executing contracts with predefined rules, to automate financial activities without the need for intermediaries like banks or traditional financial institutions.

Key characteristics of DeFi include:

1. *Decentralization:* DeFi operates on blockchain networks, which are decentralized and distributed, ensuring that financial activities are not controlled by any central authority.

2. *Open and Permissionless:* DeFi protocols are open-source, meaning anyone can access and review the code. They are also permissionless, allowing anyone with an

internet connection to participate and use DeFi applications.

3. *Interoperability:* Many DeFi projects are designed to be interoperable, enabling seamless integration and interaction between different protocols and platforms.

4. *Non-Custodial:* DeFi users retain control of their funds through non-custodial wallets, meaning they have ownership of their private keys and are not reliant on third-party custodians.

5. *Transparency:* All transactions and activities on DeFi platforms are recorded on the blockchain, making them transparent and auditable.

DEFI OFFERS A WIDE RANGE OF FINANCIAL SERVICES AND PRODUCTS, INCLUDING:

1. *Decentralized Exchanges (DEX):* DEXs facilitate peer-to-peer trading of cryptocurrencies, allowing users to exchange digital assets directly from their wallets without the need for a centralized intermediary.

2. *Decentralized Lending and Borrowing:* DeFi lending protocols enable users to lend their cryptocurrencies and earn interest or borrow assets by providing collateral.

This removes the need for traditional banks or lending institutions.

3. *Stablecoins:* DeFi has popularized the use of stablecoins, which are cryptocurrencies pegged to a stable asset like fiat currency, to provide stability within the volatile cryptocurrency market.

4. *Yield Farming:* Yield farming involves providing liquidity to DeFi protocols and earning rewards in the form of additional tokens or fees.

5. *Insurance:* DeFi insurance protocols offer coverage against potential financial losses due to smart contract vulnerabilities or hacks.

6. *Prediction Markets:* DeFi prediction markets allow users to speculate on the outcomes of various events, such as elections or sports events.

7. *Automated Market Makers (AMM):* AMMs facilitate liquidity provision and trading through algorithmic pricing models, eliminating the need for order books.

Despite the innovative potential and rapid growth of DeFi, it also comes with challenges and risks, such as smart contract vulnerabilities, price volatility, liquidity issues, and regulatory uncertainty. Users are encouraged to exercise caution, conduct thorough research, and understand the risks involved before participating in DeFi protocols. Additionally, the DeFi space continues to evolve rapidly, with new projects and improvements being introduced regularly, making it an exciting area for innovation and disruption in the financial industry.

CRYPTOCURRENCY REGULATIONS

C ryptocurrency regulations vary significantly from country to country and are influenced by factors such as the level of adoption, the government's stance on cryptocurrencies, and concerns related to consumer protection, financial stability, money laundering, and tax evasion. As of my last update in September 2021, the regulatory landscape surrounding cryptocurrencies was still evolving, and new developments may have occurred since then. Here are some key aspects of cryptocurrency regulations:

1. Regulatory Approaches:

- Prohibition: Some countries have outright banned the use and trading of cryptocurrencies. In these regions, possessing, buying, selling, or using cryptocurrencies can result in legal consequences.

- Permissive: Some countries have embraced cryptocurrencies and blockchain technology, providing a favorable regulatory environment to promote innovation and adoption.

- Restrictive: Other countries have opted for a more cautious approach, imposing restrictions and limitations on cryptocurrency activities while allowing some level of use and trading.

2. *Licensing and Registration:*

- Some countries require cryptocurrency exchanges, wallet providers, and other crypto-related businesses to obtain licenses or register with regulatory authorities to operate legally.

3. *Anti-Money Laundering (AML) and Know Your Customer (KYC):*

- Many jurisdictions impose AML and KYC requirements on cryptocurrency businesses to prevent money laundering and illicit activities. These requirements may include identity verification and transaction monitoring.

4. *Securities Regulations:*

- Cryptocurrencies and initial coin offerings (ICOs) that are deemed to be securities may be subject to securities regulations, such as registration with financial authorities and compliance with investor protection laws.

5. *Taxation:*

- Cryptocurrency transactions may be subject to taxation in some countries, and tax authorities may require individuals and businesses to report their crypto holdings and capital gains.

6. *Consumer Protection:*

- Some regulations focus on protecting consumers from fraudulent schemes, scams, and misleading information related to cryptocurrencies.

7. *Cross-Border Regulations:*

- The global nature of cryptocurrencies presents challenges for regulators. Some countries have cooperated with international efforts to establish guidelines for cross-border cryptocurrency transactions and money laundering prevention.

8. *Central Bank Digital Currencies (CBDCs):*

- Several central banks are exploring the creation of their own digital currencies, known as CBDCs, which could have implications for the regulatory landscape and the relationship between traditional fiat currencies and cryptocurrencies.

Given the complexity and evolving nature of cryptocurrency regulations, it is crucial for individuals and businesses operating in the cryptocurrency space to stay informed about the regulatory environment in their respective countries and regions. Compliance with applicable regulations is essential to avoid legal issues and ensure a safe and legitimate use of cryptocurrencies. As the crypto industry continues to develop, regulatory clarity is expected to become more defined, providing greater stability and confidence for participants in the market.

CRYPTOCURRENCY AND THE FUTURE OF FINANCE

Cryptocurrency has the potential to revolutionize the future of finance in various ways. As the crypto market and blockchain technology continue to evolve, cryptocurrencies are gaining traction as an alternative financial system that challenges traditional financial institutions and systems. Here are some ways in which cryptocurrency could shape the future of finance:

1. *Financial Inclusion:* Cryptocurrencies can provide financial services to unbanked and underbanked populations around the world, granting them access to a range of financial products without the need for traditional banks. With just an internet connection, individuals can participate in the global financial system.

2. *Borderless Transactions:* Cryptocurrencies enable fast and low-cost cross-border transactions, eliminating the need for intermediaries like banks and reducing currency

conversion fees. This can facilitate global trade and remittances, making cross-border transactions more efficient and affordable.

3. ***Decentralization and Trustlessness:*** The decentralized nature of cryptocurrencies and blockchain technology removes the need for intermediaries, such as banks and financial institutions, in financial transactions. Smart contracts and decentralized applications (dApps) can automate processes without relying on a central authority, promoting transparency and reducing the risk of manipulation.

4. ***Financial Sovereignty***: Cryptocurrencies empower individuals with full control over their funds and financial data. Users manage their private keys, ensuring they have ownership of their assets and can transact without relying on third parties.

5. ***DeFi and Decentralized Services:*** The rise of DeFi platforms provides a decentralized alternative to traditional financial services, including lending, borrowing, insurance, and asset management. DeFi protocols operate autonomously through smart contracts, offering greater accessibility and transparency.

6. ***Tokenization of Assets:*** Cryptocurrencies allow the tokenization of real-world assets, such as real estate, art, and commodities. Fractional ownership of these assets becomes possible, enabling a more diverse investment landscape.

7. ***Programmable Money:*** Smart contracts enable the automation of financial agreements, enabling programmable money that can self-execute when specific conditions are met. This can streamline complex financial processes and reduce administrative overhead.

8. ***Central Bank Digital Currencies (CBDCs):*** Some central banks are exploring the issuance of CBDCs, which are digital representations of their fiat currencies. CBDCs could improve the efficiency of monetary policies, cross-border payments, and financial stability.

9. ***Investment Opportunities:*** Cryptocurrencies have become an attractive investment class for individuals and institutional investors, offering the potential for high returns and diversification in investment portfolios.

Despite the potential benefits, the future of cryptocurrency and its impact on finance also come with challenges. These include regulatory concerns, scalability issues, market volatility, security risks, and the need for broader adoption to achieve mainstream integration. Overcoming these challenges will require ongoing collaboration between regulators, industry players, and technology developers to build a sustainable and inclusive financial ecosystem.

As the cryptocurrency space continues to mature and develop, it is likely to play an increasingly significant role in shaping the future of finance, offering innovative solutions and disrupting traditional financial paradigms. However, achieving this vision will depend on addressing regulatory hurdles, technological advancements, and building trust among users and stakeholders in the financial sector.

CRYPTOCURRENCY AND ENVIRONMENTAL CONCERNS

Cryptocurrency mining and transactions have raised environmental concerns, primarily due to the significant energy consumption associated with certain blockchain consensus mechanisms and mining processes. The environmental impact of cryptocurrencies can be attributed to the following factors:

1. *Proof-of-Work (PoW) Consensus:* PoW is the consensus mechanism used by cryptocurrencies like Bitcoin and Ethereum. In PoW, miners compete to solve complex mathematical puzzles to validate transactions and add new blocks to the blockchain. This process requires vast computational power, leading to high energy consumption.

2. *Energy-Intensive Mining:* As the difficulty of mining increases and more computational power is required, the

energy consumption of mining operations also rises. Large-scale mining farms often operate 24/7 and consume massive amounts of electricity.

3. *Carbon Emissions:* Many regions with significant mining activities rely on fossil fuels for electricity generation. This dependence on fossil fuels contributes to carbon emissions and increases the environmental impact of cryptocurrency mining.

4. *E-Waste*: The constant demand for mining hardware has led to a surge in electronic waste (e-waste) from outdated or obsolete mining equipment, further exacerbating environmental concerns.

5. *Transaction Energy Usage:* While PoW consumes substantial energy, even other consensus mechanisms like Proof-of-Stake (PoS) and Delegated Proof-of-Stake (DPoS) consume energy for transaction processing, although to a lesser extent.

EFFORTS TO MITIGATE ENVIRONMENTAL IMPACT:

1. *Renewable Energy Adoption:* Some cryptocurrency mining operations are exploring the use of renewable

energy sources, such as hydro, solar, and wind power, to reduce their carbon footprint.

2. *Transition to PoS:* Some Cryptocurrencies are transitioning from PoW to PoS consensus mechanisms, which are considered more energy-efficient. PoS require validators to hold and "stake" a certain amount of the cryptocurrency to participate in block validation, rather than competing through computations.

3. *Sustainable Mining Practices:* Miners and mining pools are exploring sustainable practices and improving energy efficiency to reduce environmental impact.

4. *Carbon Offsetting:* Some projects and companies in the crypto space are implementing carbon offset initiatives, investing in environmentally friendly projects to compensate for their carbon emissions.

5. *Energy Consumption Awareness:* Raising awareness about the energy consumption of cryptocurrencies can encourage users and stakeholders to seek greener alternatives and support energy-efficient initiatives.

Regulatory and Policy Considerations:

Environmental concerns surrounding cryptocurrencies have prompted discussions among policymakers and regulators. Some countries are exploring ways to address the energy consumption of cryptocurrencies through regulations and incentives to promote greener mining practices.

As the crypto industry continues to grow, finding a balance between innovation and sustainability will be crucial. Technology advancements, regulatory frameworks, and industry collaboration can play significant roles in addressing environmental concerns associated with cryptocurrencies and ensuring a more sustainable future for the digital asset space.

CRYPTOCURRENCY IN EVERYDAY USE

While cryptocurrencies were initially conceived as a digital asset class and investment vehicle, their use has evolved to encompass various everyday applications. As the crypto market matures, cryptocurrencies are increasingly being integrated into various aspects of daily life. Here are some ways in which cryptocurrencies are used in everyday situations:

1. *Online Shopping*: Some online retailers and e-commerce platforms accept cryptocurrencies as a form of payment. Users can use their digital wallets to make purchases, providing a convenient and secure alternative to traditional payment methods.

2. *Remittances:* Cryptocurrencies offer an efficient and cost-effective means for cross-border remittances. Users can send and receive funds globally without the need for traditional banks or intermediaries, reducing transaction fees and processing times.

3. *Micropayments:* Cryptocurrencies enable micropayments, allowing users to make small transactions for content access, online services, or digital goods without incurring significant fees.

4. *Travel and Accommodation:* In the travel industry, some airlines, hotels, and travel agencies accept cryptocurrencies as payment for flights, hotel bookings, and other travel-related services.

5. *Charitable Donations:* Cryptocurrencies are increasingly being used for charitable donations and fundraising campaigns, providing transparency and traceability for donors and beneficiaries.

6. *Gaming and Virtual Assets:* In the gaming industry, cryptocurrencies are used for in-game purchases and transactions, as well as for trading virtual assets and collectibles on blockchain-based marketplaces.

7. *Personal Finance and Investments:* Individuals use cryptocurrencies as an investment vehicle, diversifying their investment portfolios and potentially earning returns through price appreciation.

8. *Peer-to-Peer Transactions:* Cryptocurrencies enable direct peer-to-peer transactions without the need for an

intermediary, making it easy for friends and family to transfer funds to one another.

9. ***DeFi Services:*** Decentralized Finance (DeFi) platforms offer various financial services, such as lending, borrowing, and earning interest on cryptocurrencies, accessible to anyone with an internet connection.

10. ***Privacy and Security:*** Cryptocurrencies offer enhanced privacy and security compared to traditional payment methods. Transactions conducted on public blockchains are pseudonymous, meaning users can conduct transactions without revealing personal information.

It's essential to note that the adoption of cryptocurrencies in everyday life varies by region and industry. While cryptocurrencies have gained popularity, there are still challenges to overcome, such as regulatory barriers, price volatility, and scalability issues. Additionally, as the technology continues to evolve, more innovative use cases for cryptocurrencies in daily life are likely to emerge, further integrating digital assets into the mainstream economy.

CHALLENGES AND OPPORTUNITIES IN CRYPTOCURRENCY

Challenges and opportunities in the cryptocurrency space abound, as the industry continues to mature and evolve. While cryptocurrencies offer numerous benefits, they also face several challenges that need to be addressed for broader adoption and long-term sustainability. Here are some key challenges and opportunities in the cryptocurrency ecosystem:

CHALLENGES:

1. ***Regulatory Uncertainty:*** Cryptocurrencies operate in a rapidly changing regulatory landscape. The lack of clear and consistent regulations across jurisdictions creates uncertainty for businesses and users, potentially hindering mainstream adoption.

2. *Security Risks:* Cybersecurity threats, such as hacking, phishing, and scams, pose significant risks to cryptocurrency holders and exchanges. High-profile security breaches can erode trust in the industry.

3. *Price Volatility:* Cryptocurrencies are known for their price volatility, which can lead to speculative bubbles and market instability, deterring some potential users from participating.

4. *Scalability:* Many blockchain networks face scalability issues, struggling to handle a large number of transactions in a timely and cost-effective manner. This can lead to slow transaction processing and higher fees during peak usage times.

5. *Energy Consumption:* Certain consensus mechanisms, like Proof-of-Work, are energy-intensive and have raised concerns about the environmental impact of cryptocurrency mining.

6. *Lack of Education:* The complexity of blockchain technology and cryptocurrencies can be a barrier to entry for newcomers. A lack of understanding and education may lead to misinformation and misguided investments.

OPPORTUNITIES:

1. *Financial Inclusion:* Cryptocurrencies can provide financial services to the unbanked and underbanked populations, granting access to financial tools and services without traditional banking infrastructure.

2. *Decentralized Finance (DeFi):* DeFi platforms offer innovative financial services, enabling users to access lending, borrowing, and yield farming directly through smart contracts, removing the need for intermediaries.

3. *Tokenization of Assets:* Cryptocurrencies enable the tokenization of real-world assets, such as real estate and commodities, allowing for fractional ownership and increased liquidity in traditionally illiquid markets.

4. *Cross-Border Transactions:* Cryptocurrencies offer a seamless and low-cost solution for cross-border payments and remittances, potentially improving efficiency and reducing fees compared to traditional methods.

5. *Programmable Money:* Smart contracts enable the automation of financial agreements, potentially streamlining complex processes and reducing administrative costs.

6. ***Central Bank Digital Currencies (CBDCs):*** The development of CBDCs by central banks could enhance monetary policy and facilitate digital payments while offering opportunities for integration with traditional financial systems.

7. ***Innovation and Research:*** The cryptocurrency space continues to be a hub of innovation, with ongoing research and development focusing on scalability solutions, privacy enhancements, and interoperability between blockchain networks.

Addressing the challenges and embracing the opportunities will require collaboration among industry stakeholders, regulators, and the broader community. Regulatory clarity, improved security measures, scalable solutions, and enhanced education can contribute to the sustainable growth and positive impact of cryptocurrencies in the global financial landscape. As the technology advances and new use cases emerge, cryptocurrencies have the potential to reshape finance and disrupt traditional systems, opening up a world of possibilities for financial inclusion and innovation.

CRYPTOCURRENCY IN THE MEDIA AND PUBLIC PERCEPTION

Cryptocurrencies have garnered significant attention in the media and have evoked diverse public perceptions since their inception. The coverage and portrayal of cryptocurrencies in the media can greatly influence public opinion and understanding of this nascent technology. Here are some key aspects related to cryptocurrency in the media and public perception:

1. *Media Coverage*: Cryptocurrencies have often been subject to extensive media coverage, especially during periods of extreme price volatility or significant developments in the crypto space. News outlets report on price movements, market trends, regulatory developments, and notable events related to cryptocurrencies and blockchain technology.

2. *Positive Perception:* Some media outlets and individuals view cryptocurrencies positively, emphasizing their potential to revolutionize finance, promote financial inclusion, and drive technological innovation. Positive narratives often highlight success stories, use cases, and the transformative impact of cryptocurrencies.

3. *Negative Perception:* On the other hand, cryptocurrencies have also faced criticism in the media. Negative coverage may focus on price volatility, scams, hacking incidents, regulatory concerns, and environmental issues related to cryptocurrency mining.

4. *Volatility and Speculation:* Cryptocurrencies' inherent price volatility can lead to sensationalized headlines in the media, portraying the market as highly speculative and risky. Extreme price fluctuations can attract both positive and negative attention, with headlines often emphasizing potential gains or losses.

5. *Lack of Understanding:* Cryptocurrencies' technical complexities can be challenging for the general public to grasp fully. This lack of understanding can

lead to misconceptions, skepticism, or fear of the unknown, further influencing public perception.

6. *Pop Culture References:* Cryptocurrencies have increasingly become a part of popular culture, featured in movies, TV shows, and even songs. Such references can influence public perception, but they may not always provide an accurate depiction of cryptocurrencies and their potential.

7. *Impact on Investment Decisions:* Media coverage can influence investment decisions, especially among retail investors. Positive or negative news can trigger mass buying or selling of cryptocurrencies, contributing to price fluctuations.

8. *Regulatory Developments:* Coverage of regulatory actions or statements from government officials can impact public perception. Clarity and consistency in regulatory frameworks can enhance confidence in cryptocurrencies.

9. *Education Efforts:* Some media outlets and experts strive to educate the public about cryptocurrencies, providing accurate information, explanations of technology, and analyses of market trends.

INFLUENCING PUBLIC PERCEPTION:

Public perception of cryptocurrencies can shape their adoption and acceptance in mainstream society. To improve public understanding, it's essential for media outlets, industry leaders, and educators to prioritize accurate reporting and educational initiatives. Additionally, transparency and responsible communication from cryptocurrency projects can foster trust among the public.

Public perception may continue to evolve as the cryptocurrency industry matures and experiences technological advancements, regulatory developments, and increased use cases. As the technology becomes more integrated into everyday life, accurate and unbiased reporting will play a vital role in shaping public opinion and understanding of cryptocurrencies and blockchain technology.

NON-FUNGIBLE TOKENS (NFTs)

NFTs, or Non-Fungible Tokens, are unique digital assets that represent ownership or proof of authenticity of a specific item or piece of content. Unlike cryptocurrencies such as Bitcoin or Ethereum, which are interchangeable, NFTs are one-of-a-kind.

Digital Ownership: NFTs introduce a groundbreaking paradigm of establishing ownership within the digital realm, fundamentally altering our perceptions of digital assets. We'll embark on an exploration of this profound shift in the concept of possession, where individuals can claim authentic ownership of a diverse array of digital entities. This spans the spectrum from exquisite digital artworks and cherished collectibles to virtual real estate holdings in metaverse landscapes, and surprisingly, even the ownership rights to a mere tweet. Here we will unravel the transformative power of NFTs in providing unequivocal digital ownership across these diverse domains, shedding light on the exciting possibilities and challenges that lie ahead in this emerging landscape.

THE TECHNOLOGY BEHIND NFTs

Blockchain Backbone: NFTs, as a groundbreaking concept, find their very foundation in the revolutionary technology of blockchain. It's essential to delve into the intricate workings of this underlying technology to comprehend how NFTs attain their uniqueness and provenance. Blockchain, at its core, is a decentralized and transparent ledger system, serving as a tamper-proof, unforgeable record of all transactions. In our exploration, we will elucidate the profound significance of this blockchain technology.

The transparency of blockchain ensures that every NFT's entire transaction history is visible to anyone, at any time. It's a meticulous and immutable chronicle of ownership transfers and changes, enabling anyone to trace the journey of an NFT from its creation to its current possessor. We'll highlight how this transparency fosters trust and authenticity in the NFT space, assuring buyers and creators of the genuine nature of the digital asset.

The security aspect is equally pivotal. Blockchain's decentralized architecture, achieved through a network of nodes that validate and record transactions, fortifies the NFT ecosystem against fraudulent activities. Any unauthorized attempts to alter the blockchain's data are thwarted, ensuring the integrity of NFT ownership records. As a result, we'll underscore how blockchain instills confidence in NFT transactions, safeguarding them against unauthorized alterations or counterfeit claims.

In essence, blockchain technology's role in NFTs is akin to a digital notary, providing an indelible proof of the uniqueness and provenance of each NFT. This chapter will shed light on the intricate interplay between blockchain and NFTs, offering a comprehensive understanding of the technology that underpins the digital ownership revolution.

Smart Contracts: Smart contracts, a cornerstone of the NFT ecosystem, play a central and transformative role in the world of digital ownership. It's crucial to dissect the intricate mechanisms of smart contracts to comprehend how they facilitate automated ownership transfers and royalties, all while ensuring creators maintain a vested interest in the prosperity of their work.

These ingenious pieces of code are essentially self-executing contracts with predefined rules and conditions. In the context of NFTs, smart contracts serve as the digital custodians of ownership rights. As we delve into their functioning, we'll witness how these contracts autonomously execute the transfer of NFT ownership from one party to another as soon as the agreed-upon conditions are met. This automated process eliminates the need for intermediaries, making NFT transactions swift and efficient.

When an NFT changes hands in a secondary market, the smart contract can be programmed to automatically allocate a percentage of the sale price to the original creator. This revolutionary feature ensures that artists, musicians, or any content creators receive a continuous stake in the success of their work. We'll delve into various models of royalty distribution and how this empowers creators by providing ongoing compensation for their creations' growing value. It's a testament to the power of technology in revolutionizing the art of ownership and empowering creators in the digital age.

NFT APPLICATIONS

Art and Collectibles: The transformative impact of NFTs on the art world is nothing short of revolutionary. To truly grasp this paradigm shift, we must explore how NFTs are redefining the art landscape, with artists and collectors enthusiastically adopting the concept of digital ownership. The art community has witnessed remarkable NFT art sales, with some digital artworks commanding extraordinary prices. These sales have disrupted traditional norms in the art world, fundamentally altering the landscape of art ownership, creation, and appreciation. This convergence of art and technology represents a significant paradigm shift, offering both artists and collectors unique opportunities in the digital age. In technical terms, the merger of art and NFTs primarily relies on the integration of blockchain technology and smart contracts. Here's how it works:

1. *Blockchain Technology:* NFTs are built on blockchain platforms, which are decentralized, distributed ledgers. Each digital artwork is represented by a unique NFT, and its ownership history is recorded on the blockchain. This ensures transparency and immutability, preventing unauthorized alterations. The blockchain serves as a ledger of ownership.

2. *Smart Contracts:* Smart contracts are self-executing pieces of code that run on blockchain platforms like Ethereum. They contain predefined rules and conditions for NFT transactions. When someone purchases an NFT, the smart contract automatically transfers ownership to the buyer and records the transaction on the blockchain.

3. *Tokenization:* Artists tokenize their digital artwork by creating an NFT. This process involves minting a new NFT that represents the artwork. The NFT contains

metadata, including details about the artwork, provenance, and ownership information.

4. *Ownership Transfer:* When a collector buys an NFT, the smart contract transfers ownership of the NFT to the collector. The ownership change is reflected on the blockchain, ensuring transparency and proof of ownership.

5. *Royalties and Secondary Sales:* Smart contracts can be programmed to include royalties for the original artist. When the NFT is resold in a secondary market, a percentage of the sale price is automatically sent to the artist's wallet, providing an ongoing revenue stream for creators.

6. *Interoperability:* NFTs can be created on various blockchain platforms, but the most common is Ethereum. Interoperable standards like ERC-721 and ERC-1155 ensure that NFTs can be bought, sold, and displayed across different marketplaces and platforms.

7. *Wallet Integration:* Collectors and artists use cryptocurrency wallets to manage their NFTs. These wallets enable them to buy, sell, and transfer NFTs. Wallets also facilitate the display and storage of NFT art.

8. *Marketplaces and Platforms:* NFT art is showcased and traded on online marketplaces and platforms designed

specifically for NFTs. These platforms connect artists with collectors and provide a user-friendly interface for minting, buying, and selling NFTs.

Gaming and Virtual Worlds: NFTs have made their way into the gaming world, revolutionizing how players interact with virtual environments. They empower players to truly own in-game assets, from valuable items to virtual properties, reshaping the gaming landscape.

With NFTs, players gain real ownership of their in-game possessions, enabling them to trade, buy, and sell digital assets within a virtual marketplace. This transformation challenges conventional views of virtual property rights and introduces significant shifts in the dynamics of in-game economies.

The impact extends beyond ownership to gameplay itself. NFTs bring the potential for cross-game interoperability, allowing players to carry their cherished in-game assets and characters across various virtual worlds. This newfound mobility and interoperability are redefining gaming experiences, offering a level of personalization and uniqueness previously unattainable.

In summary, NFTs in gaming represent a pivotal shift where players transcend their roles as mere participants to become genuine digital property owners in an ever-evolving gaming environment. The consequences encompass property rights, in-game economies, and gameplay dynamics, providing a glimpse into the future of immersive virtual worlds.

Music and Entertainment: NFTs have permeated the music and entertainment industry, ushering in a new era of engagement between musicians, content creators, and their audiences. This transformation showcases the innovative ways in which NFTs are redefining the relationship between artists and fans.

Musicians and content creators are leveraging NFTs to engage with their audience in unprecedented ways. They can mint NFTs representing exclusive music tracks, concert tickets, or unique behind-the-scenes content. These NFTs serve as digital collectibles, providing fans with a tangible connection to their favorite artists.

Moreover, NFTs offer a novel approach to monetization. Musicians can directly sell their music or merchandise to fans as NFTs, eliminating intermediaries and providing a new revenue stream. NFTs also enable artists to incorporate royalties into their digital creations, ensuring that they continue to benefit from their work's success.

CREATING AND OWNING NFTs

The Minting Process: Creators embark on the journey of turning their work into Non-Fungible Tokens (NFTs) by first digitizing their art, music, or other digital content. This involves transforming their creations into a digital format, which could be a high-resolution image, a 3D model, a sound file, or any other form of digital representation. For creators dealing with physical art, this often requires creating a high-quality digital version that accurately mirrors the original work.

The next step in the process is minting the NFT, and this is where blockchain technology comes into play. Creators typically use NFT marketplaces like OpenSea, Rarible, or Mintable to mint their NFTs. To do this, they need a digital wallet that is compatible with the chosen marketplace to store and manage their NFTs. Within the marketplace, creators initiate the minting process, which involves uploading the digital file representing their work and providing essential metadata. This metadata includes information such as the title of the work, a detailed description, and any unique attributes that make the NFT special.

Once the digital file and metadata are in place, creators have the flexibility to determine ownership and licensing options.

They can choose to mint NFTs as one-of-a-kind (1/1) tokens, emphasizing the uniqueness of their work, or they can opt for multiple editions, each with a specific quantity, allowing for broader ownership. Additionally, creators can set specific licenses that define the terms of use for their NFTs. These licenses may encompass personal or commercial use, outlining the rights and restrictions associated with the NFT.

Minting NFTs involves the payment of gas fees, which are transaction costs on the blockchain network. Creators are responsible for covering these fees, and the amount can vary depending on the network's congestion and the complexity of the NFT. After confirming the minting process, the NFT is created on the blockchain, and a unique token ID is generated. This token ID is crucial for distinguishing one NFT from another and tracking its ownership and transaction history on the blockchain. Once minted, creators have the option to list their NFTs on various NFT marketplaces, making them accessible to potential buyers. They can set fixed prices for immediate purchase or define reserve prices for auction-style listings. Additionally, creators can specify royalties for secondary sales, ensuring they receive a percentage of the sale price when their NFT is resold in the future. Promotion and marketing play a vital role in the NFT journey. Creators often utilize social media, art communities, and their own websites to generate visibility for their NFTs. Collaborations with influencers and participation in NFT drops and events are common strategies to attract potential buyers. Once a buyer acquires an NFT, ownership is transferred to their digital wallet. The blockchain records the NFT's provenance and transaction history, creating a transparent and immutable ledger of ownership. By meticulously following these steps, creators can effectively transform their creative work into NFTs, making them accessible to a global audience of collectors and enthusiasts. This process combines the realms of technology, creativity, and entrepreneurial spirit, opening doors to the growing and dynamic NFT market.

Wallets and Storage: Cryptocurrency wallets play a crucial role in securely storing Non-Fungible Tokens (NFTs) and asserting ownership over these unique digital assets. NFTs are built on blockchain technology, and they are often stored in compatible cryptocurrency wallets that support the blockchain on which the NFT was minted. These wallets act as digital containers for NFTs, safeguarding them against unauthorized access and providing a secure environment for ownership assertion.

One of the primary functions of cryptocurrency wallets is to provide a secure storage space for NFTs. NFTs represent ownership and authenticity of digital assets, and losing access to them can have significant consequences. Cryptocurrency wallets utilize encryption and private keys to protect the NFTs stored within them. Private keys are long alphanumeric strings that serve as digital signatures, ensuring that only the wallet owner has control over the NFTs. Wallets come in various forms, including software wallets, hardware wallets, and paper wallets, each offering different levels of security and accessibility to cater to a user's specific needs and preferences.

In addition to secure storage, cryptocurrency wallets are instrumental in the process of asserting ownership over NFTs. When an NFT is purchased or transferred, the ownership records are updated on the blockchain. Cryptocurrency wallets play a critical role in managing these transactions by providing the private keys required to initiate transfers. This process confirms the ownership of the NFT and the rightful control over its future use or transfer. Ownership assertion is not only about securing the NFT but also about having the ability to make decisions regarding its sale, display, or use in virtual environments.

The choice of cryptocurrency wallet can significantly impact the security and ownership assertion of NFTs. Users should carefully select a wallet that aligns with their preferences and risk tolerance. Software wallets are accessible and user-friendly, making them suitable for everyday use. Hardware wallets, on the other hand, offer enhanced security through physical devices that store private keys offline. Paper wallets provide an extra layer of security by generating physical documents with private key information. Understanding the different options and their security features is crucial for users to confidently and securely store and assert ownership over their NFTs.

In essence, the importance of cryptocurrency wallets in the realm of NFTs cannot be overstated. These wallets serve as both fortresses for secure storage and gateways for asserting ownership. The use of encryption, private keys, and various wallet types ensures that NFTs remain protected and under the control of their rightful owners, fostering trust and confidence in the NFT ecosystem.

NFT MARKETPLACES AND TRADING

Prominent Marketplaces: These platforms have played a pivotal role in the NFT space, each with its unique features and offerings.

OpenSea: OpenSea stands as one of the most prominent and widely recognized NFT marketplaces. It's known for its vast and diverse collection of NFTs, including digital art, collectibles, virtual real estate, and more. OpenSea offers an intuitive interface, allowing users to browse, buy, and sell NFTs seamlessly. One of its standout features is its support for Ethereum-based NFTs, making it a go-to platform for Ethereum enthusiasts. It has become a hub for artists, creators, and collectors, making it a vibrant marketplace in the NFT ecosystem.

Rarible: Rarible is another popular NFT marketplace with a unique twist—it's a decentralized platform that allows users to create their own NFTs. This feature, known as "minting," empowers artists and creators to turn their digital content into NFTs and list them for sale. Rarible's governance token, RARI, plays a significant role in the platform's decentralized operations. The marketplace is home to a variety of NFTs, and it has gained recognition for its community-driven approach, making it a hub for both creators and collectors.

SuperRare: SuperRare is a premium NFT marketplace that specializes in digital art. It's a platform where artists showcase and sell their unique, limited-edition digital artworks. Each piece is tokenized as an NFT, emphasizing its scarcity and authenticity. SuperRare has gained a reputation for attracting renowned digital artists and collectors. It incorporates a social element, allowing users to follow their favorite artists and engage in a community that revolves around digital art appreciation.

These are just a few of the prominent NFT marketplaces, each offering distinct experiences and opportunities for both creators and collectors. As the NFT ecosystem continues to evolve, more marketplaces and platforms are emerging, catering to different niches and preferences within the NFT space. These marketplaces exemplify the dynamic and diverse nature of the NFT market, where digital assets are bought, sold, and celebrated by a global community of enthusiasts.

Trading Dynamics: Here's details on trading mechanisms for NFTs, from auctions to fixed-price sales, and provide real-world examples of significant NFT transactions.

Auctions: NFT auctions are similar to traditional auctions but take place in the digital realm. Sellers set a starting price, and potential buyers place bids. The NFT is awarded to the highest bidder when the auction concludes. Auctions can be timed, with a set duration, or untimed, allowing the seller to choose when to end the bidding.

Fixed-Price Sales: In fixed-price sales, NFTs are listed with a set purchase price. Buyers can instantly purchase the NFT at the listed price without the need for bidding. This mechanism offers a straightforward and immediate way to acquire NFTs.

Dutch Auctions: Dutch auctions begin with a high asking price, which gradually decreases over time. Buyers can choose to purchase the NFT at any point during the auction. The first buyer to accept the current price secures the NFT. This approach encourages quick decision-making.

Real-World Examples of Significant NFT Transactions:

➤ Beeple's "Everydays: The First 5000 Days":
- Mechanism: Auction
- Transaction: This digital artwork by Beeple (Mike Winkelmann) was sold at a Christie's auction in March 2021. It became one of the most expensive NFTs ever sold, with a final price of $69.3 million.

- ➢ CryptoPunk #7804:
- • Mechanism: Fixed-Price Sale
- • Transaction: CryptoPunk #7804, one of the 10,000 unique 24x24 pixel art characters, was sold for 4200 ETH (over $7 million at the time) in a fixed-price sale on Larva Labs' marketplace.

- ➢ CryptoKitties' "Dragon" NFT:
- • Mechanism: Dutch Auction
- • Transaction: CryptoKitties, a popular NFT project, introduced a Dutch auction for their "Dragon" NFT. The price started at 300 ETH and decreased by 10% every 24 hours. The NFT was eventually sold for approximately 600 ETH.

CHALLENGES AND CONTROVERSIES

Environmental Concerns: The debate surrounding the energy consumption of Non-Fungible Tokens (NFTs) and their impact on the environment is a topic of significant concern and discussion within the NFT community and the broader public. This debate revolves around several key points:

1. Energy Consumption of NFTs:

One of the primary concerns is the substantial energy consumption associated with some NFT transactions. NFTs are often built on blockchain networks, with Ethereum being a commonly used platform. These networks rely on a consensus mechanism called Proof of Work (PoW), which requires miners to solve complex mathematical puzzles to validate and record transactions on the blockchain. This process, while secure, consumes a considerable amount of energy.

2. Carbon Footprint:

Critics argue that the energy-intensive nature of PoW blockchains, such as Ethereum, results in a substantial carbon footprint. The energy consumption and associated emissions have raised concerns about the environmental impact of NFTs, particularly in a time when there is a growing emphasis on sustainability and reducing carbon emissions.

3. Efforts to Address Concerns:

In response to these concerns, some NFT platforms and artists are actively seeking more environmentally friendly alternatives. Ethereum itself is in the process of transitioning from PoW to Proof of Stake (PoS), a consensus mechanism that requires significantly less energy. PoS has the potential to reduce the environmental impact of NFT transactions.

4. Offsetting Carbon Emissions:

Some NFT creators and marketplaces are taking proactive steps to offset the carbon emissions generated by their NFT activities. They are investing in carbon offset projects and environmentally conscious initiatives to mitigate the environmental impact of NFTs.

5. Balancing Environmental Concerns with Innovation:

The NFT community acknowledges the environmental concerns and is actively exploring ways to balance innovation with environmental responsibility. The debate underscores the need to find sustainable solutions that align with the evolving NFT landscape.

The debate surrounding NFTs and their environmental impact emphasizes the growing importance of considering sustainability in blockchain technology. It encourages stakeholders to seek more eco-friendly alternatives and to take responsibility for the carbon footprint of their NFT activities. This debate is likely to continue as the NFT space evolves, with an increasing emphasis on finding solutions that benefit both creators and the environment.

Copyright and Plagiarism: NFTs have indeed sparked copyright debates, and several cases of plagiarism and copyright infringement within the NFT space have drawn significant attention. Here are some notable examples:

1. CryptoPunks Copycats:

Case: CryptoPunks, a popular NFT project, has witnessed numerous cases of copycat projects attempting to replicate or imitate the original 10,000 unique 24x24 pixel art characters.

Issue: These copycat projects raise concerns about intellectual property rights and the originality of NFT collections. Some of these projects may infringe on the copyrights of the original creators, Larva Labs.

2. Art Plagiarism on Rarible:

Case: Rarible, a decentralized NFT marketplace, has faced issues with artists plagiarizing the works of others and minting them as their own NFTs for sale.

Issue: This highlights the challenge of verifying the authenticity and originality of digital art in the NFT space. It raises questions about the responsibility of NFT marketplaces in preventing copyright infringement.

3. Beeple's Stolen Artwork:

Case: Renowned digital artist Beeple (Mike Winkelmann) reported that one of his digital artworks was stolen, minted as an NFT, and listed for sale without his consent.

Issue: This case underscores the vulnerability of artists' digital creations to theft and unauthorized minting as NFTs. It also emphasizes the need for robust copyright protection in the NFT ecosystem.

4. Copyright Claims on NBA Top Shot:

Case: NBA Top Shot, an NFT platform featuring officially licensed NBA highlights, has faced copyright claims from players and their representatives. Some NFT moments have been removed due to intellectual property disputes.

Issue: The case highlights the complexity of licensing and copyright in the NFT space, especially when dealing with widely recognized intellectual property like sports highlights.

5. Music Copyright Infringement:

Case: NFTs related to music have been the subject of copyright disputes. Some artists have claimed that their music was used without permission in NFT projects.

Issue: This raises issues related to the use of copyrighted music in NFTs and the necessity of proper licensing and copyright compliance.

These cases of plagiarism and copyright infringement in the NFT space underscore the importance of addressing intellectual property rights and authenticity. They also highlight the need for clear guidelines and mechanisms to protect artists, creators, and collectors in the evolving NFT ecosystem. NFT platforms and marketplaces are continually working to enhance verification and copyright protection measures to maintain the integrity of the space.

FUTURE PROSPECTS

The Metaverse and Beyond: Non-Fungible Tokens (NFTs) are poised to play a transformative role in shaping the metaverse and virtual reality, with the potential to redefine our digital experiences. Here's a glimpse of how NFTs are contributing to this evolution:

1. **Digital Asset Ownership in Virtual Worlds:**

NFTs enable true ownership of digital assets, including virtual real estate, avatars, and in-game items within virtual worlds. This ownership extends beyond the confines of a specific game or metaverse platform. NFT holders can carry their digital assets across different virtual environments, creating a seamless and personalized experience. As NFT adoption grows, users will have the freedom to personalize and monetize their virtual presence, unlocking new levels of immersion in the metaverse.

2. Interoperability and Cross-Platform Experiences:

NFTs are designed to be interoperable. This means that NFTs minted on one blockchain can potentially be used in different metaverse platforms and virtual reality experiences. As more metaverse projects and virtual reality spaces emerge, NFTs will serve as a common thread, allowing users to carry their assets, identity, and achievements across different digital realms. This interoperability promises to connect and expand the metaverse ecosystem, enriching our digital experiences.

3. Digital Identity and Personal Branding:

NFTs can represent more than just virtual objects; they can embody aspects of a user's digital identity and personal brand. Virtual fashion, wearables, and accessories in the form of NFTs allow users to express themselves uniquely within the metaverse. These digital items can become status symbols and statements of individuality, shaping how users perceive and present themselves in the digital realm.

4. Content Creation and Monetization:

Artists, musicians, and content creators are finding new avenues for monetization in the metaverse through NFTs. They can mint and sell digital art, music, or virtual experiences as NFTs, retaining a continuous stake in their work's success. This creator-centric model empowers artists and encourages the production of unique and engaging content, enriching the metaverse with diverse experiences.

5. Collectibles and Virtual Communities:

NFTs facilitate the creation of virtual collectibles and the formation of communities within the metaverse. Collectors can acquire NFTs representing limited-edition items, digital pets, or even virtual land. These collectibles foster a sense of community and shared experiences within the metaverse, and they can appreciate in value over time.

As NFTs continue to permeate the metaverse and virtual reality, they hold the promise of reshaping the digital landscape. Users will navigate a virtual world where ownership, personalization, and creativity are at the forefront, offering a more immersive and engaging digital existence. With NFTs as the bridge connecting virtual experiences, the metaverse is set to become an interconnected and dynamic environment, opening up endless possibilities for exploration and interaction.

Regulatory Landscape: The regulatory framework for Non-Fungible Tokens (NFTs) is evolving, and it carries significant implications for the NFT ecosystem. Here's an overview of the key developments and their impact:

1. Intellectual Property Rights:

Implication: NFTs have raised concerns regarding copyright and intellectual property rights. Regulations may require artists and creators to prove ownership and authenticity, leading to improved copyright protection for NFT-based digital assets.

2. Securities Regulations:

Implication: Some NFTs, especially those linked to investment opportunities or revenue-sharing, may be classified as securities by regulators. This could lead to more stringent compliance requirements and restrictions on their sale and trading.

3. Anti-Money Laundering (AML) and Know Your Customer (KYC) Regulations:

Implication: NFT marketplaces and platforms may be subject to AML and KYC regulations, requiring them to implement identity verification procedures for users. This ensures transparency and compliance with financial regulations.

4. Taxation:

Implication: Tax authorities are increasingly scrutinizing NFT transactions. NFT sales, purchases, and trading may be subject to capital gains tax, VAT, or other forms of taxation, depending on the jurisdiction. Clear tax regulations will provide clarity to NFT market participants.

5. Environmental Concerns:

Implication: The energy consumption of NFTs, especially those minted on energy-intensive blockchains, may lead to environmental regulations or carbon offset requirements. NFT platforms and creators may need to account for their carbon footprint.

6. Consumer Protection:

Implication: Regulations may be introduced to protect NFT buyers from fraud, misleading descriptions, and misrepresentations. This can enhance trust in the NFT market by holding sellers accountable.

7. Cross-Border Transactions:

Implication: NFTs often transcend national boundaries, making international regulatory coordination essential. Regulations for cross-border NFT transactions, such as import and export restrictions, may be developed.

8. Gaming and Virtual Assets:

Implication: Virtual in-game assets, often represented as NFTs, raise questions about their legal status. Regulators may define their treatment in gaming environments and their potential impact on players.

9. NFT Marketplaces:

Implication: NFT marketplaces are likely to face increased regulatory scrutiny. They may need to ensure compliance with various regulations, including AML, KYC, and tax reporting, making their operations more complex.

10. Decentralized Autonomous Organizations (DAOs):

Implication: NFT-based DAOs are gaining traction. Regulatory clarity on their legal status and taxation could affect the growth and adoption of decentralized governance models.

11. Blockchain Technology:

Implication: Blockchain technology underpins NFTs, and regulatory developments related to blockchain may indirectly impact NFTs. Clarity on blockchain regulations can create a more stable environment for NFTs.

As the regulatory landscape for NFTs continues to take shape, it is essential for market participants, including artists, creators, collectors, and platforms, to stay informed and comply with relevant laws. Clear regulations can offer legitimacy to the NFT ecosystem, protect stakeholders, and encourage broader adoption while addressing concerns about security, taxation, and consumer protection. NFTs are at the intersection of innovation and regulation, and striking the right balance is crucial for their sustained growth and integration into mainstream economies.

CONCLUSION

Non-Fungible Tokens (NFTs) have ushered in a profound digital ownership revolution, leaving an indelible mark on various industries, including art, gaming, music, and beyond. While NFTs come with their set of challenges and controversies, they hold the promise of a future where the concept of digital ownership transcends conventional boundaries.

The NFT Revolution: Redefining Ownership in the Digital Age

NFTs have disrupted the way we perceive and exercise ownership in the digital realm. Unlike traditional digital assets, NFTs grant individuals true ownership of unique, verifiable, and provably scarce digital items. Whether it's a digital artwork, a rare in-game collectible, or a piece of music, NFTs empower creators and collectors to assert their ownership rights securely on the blockchain. This revolution challenges the long-standing notion that digital assets lack intrinsic value and permanence.

Exploring NFT Origins: From CryptoKitties to the Mainstream

The chapter delves into the origins of NFTs, starting with notable early projects like CryptoKitties. It outlines the evolution of NFTs, from niche blockchain communities to widespread adoption across various domains. NFTs have not only found their place in the art world but have also extended their influence to virtual gaming, music streaming, and even virtual real estate. This chapter offers insights into the journey that brought NFTs into the mainstream spotlight.

NFTs in the Art World: Beyond the Physical Canvas

NFTs have taken the art world by storm, providing artists with a groundbreaking platform to showcase, sell, and profit from their digital creations. The chapter discusses key moments in NFT art sales, including record-breaking auctions and the emergence of digital art as a legitimate and valuable form of artistic expression. It highlights how NFTs have democratized art, offering artists new avenues for exposure and revenue.

NFTs in Gaming: Owning Virtual Worlds

Virtual gaming and NFTs have converged to create a dynamic landscape where players can genuinely own in-game assets, virtual real estate, and rare collectibles. This section examines how NFTs are reshaping the gaming experience, enabling players to buy, sell, and trade their digital possessions across different gaming universes. Gamers have become virtual property owners, blurring the lines between virtual and physical ownership.

NFTs in Music: A New Era of Engagement

The chapter also explores how musicians and content creators are leveraging NFTs to engage with their audience and explore innovative revenue streams. Musicians can mint NFTs representing exclusive music releases, concert tickets, or access to VIP experiences. NFTs empower artists to establish a more direct connection with their fanbase, reshape the music industry's business model, and revolutionize digital ownership in the context of music.

Challenges and Controversies: Navigating the NFT Ecosystem

While NFTs promise a revolutionary digital future, they are not without their share of challenges. This section delves into the controversies surrounding NFTs, including concerns about energy consumption, copyright infringement, and the speculative nature of the NFT market. It also addresses how the NFT ecosystem is actively working to address these issues and establish a more sustainable and ethical framework.

The Promise of Limitless Digital Ownership

In conclusion, the chapter paints a compelling picture of a digital future where NFTs play a central role in redefining the concept of ownership. It illustrates how NFTs offer boundless possibilities across diverse industries and how they may become an integral part of our digital lives. As NFTs continue to evolve, they are set to shape a future where the boundaries of ownership extend far beyond the physical world, opening up new horizons for creators, collectors, and digital enthusiasts.

CRYPTOCURRNCY AND SPACE EXPLORATION

The intersection of cryptocurrency and space exploration is a fascinating and rapidly evolving field. Let's explore this broader topic:

CRYPTOCURRENCY FOR SPACE EXPLORATION FUNDING:

Cryptocurrency has introduced a groundbreaking approach to financing space exploration initiatives, with space agencies and private aerospace companies at the forefront of this innovative funding trend. The acceptance of cryptocurrency donations and investments for space projects has ushered in a new era of financial support for ambitious missions, offering several distinct advantages.

One of the primary advantages is the decentralized nature of cryptocurrencies, which aligns seamlessly with the principles of space exploration. Space agencies and private companies can leverage the global reach of cryptocurrencies to facilitate fundraising efforts that transcend geographical boundaries. This means that supporters from various corners of the world can participate in financing space missions, fostering a sense of inclusivity and international collaboration.

The utilization of cryptocurrencies in space funding also enhances the transparency and security of financial transactions. Blockchain technology, which underpins most cryptocurrencies, provides an immutable and auditable ledger of all transactions. This ensures that every donation or investment is traceable and accounted for, instilling a high level of trust among contributors.

Additionally, cryptocurrencies offer a level of financial inclusivity that traditional funding methods may not provide. They enable microtransactions, allowing individuals to contribute even small amounts toward space exploration projects. This opens the door for a broader community of space enthusiasts, from casual supporters to dedicated advocates, to actively participate in advancing the frontiers of space science and technology.

The use of cryptocurrency in funding space exploration is a testament to the adaptability and versatility of blockchain-based digital assets. As space agencies and private companies increasingly explore the cosmos, they are also pioneering new financial frontiers, where cryptocurrencies are integral to realizing the next generation of ambitious space missions. This synergy between cryptocurrency and space exploration not only democratizes participation but also exemplifies the collaborative and innovative spirit of the space community.

SPACE-BASED CRYPTOCURRENCY TRANSACTIONS

As humanity ventures beyond the confines of Earth and into the vast expanse of space, the need for a reliable and decentralized financial system becomes increasingly crucial. This need has given rise to the innovative concept of conducting cryptocurrency transactions in space, an idea that is rapidly gaining traction within the space exploration community. The reasons behind this emerging trend are both practical and forward-thinking.

The practical aspect revolves around the challenges associated with conducting financial transactions beyond Earth's atmosphere. Traditional banking systems are ill-equipped to handle transactions that span the cosmos, and the time delays, fees, and complexity involved in interplanetary financial activities can be staggering. Cryptocurrencies, with their inherent resilience and decentralized nature, offer an elegant solution to these challenges.

Cryptocurrencies are uniquely suited to function in remote and extreme environments, characteristics that make them ideal for space-based transactions. Their decentralized nature means they operate without reliance on a central authority or intermediary, which can be a game-changer when dealing with complex, cross-border transactions between spacecraft, space colonies, or even with extraterrestrial entities. The trust and security of blockchain technology, which underpins cryptocurrencies, make them well-suited to ensuring the integrity of space-based financial systems.

In addition to overcoming immediate practical challenges, the concept of interplanetary cryptocurrency transactions is a forward-thinking endeavor. As humanity continues to explore the cosmos and establish settlements on celestial bodies such as the Moon and Mars, the need for a robust and scalable financial system becomes even more apparent. Cryptocurrencies provide the foundation for creating a versatile, borderless, and resilient financial system that can adapt to the evolving needs of space exploration.

The idea of conducting cryptocurrency transactions in space serves as a testament to human ingenuity and adaptability. It not only streamlines the financial aspects of space exploration but also lays the groundwork for a future where digital currencies seamlessly connect Earth and the far reaches of our universe. This visionary approach aligns with the spirit of exploration and innovation that defines our journey into space, marking a significant step towards creating an interconnected interstellar economy.

LUNAR AND MARTIAN CRYPTOCURRENCY INITIATIVES:

The Moon and Mars have emerged as prime targets for human exploration, and the vision of establishing colonies on these celestial bodies is evolving from science fiction to a concrete, near-future possibility. As we prepare to extend our presence beyond Earth, one of the intriguing and forward-looking aspects of these off-world endeavors involves the exploration of cryptocurrency projects tailored for lunar and Martian habitats. These digital currencies are envisioned to serve as the backbone of a new financial ecosystem in these extraterrestrial settlements, facilitating commerce and economic activities in ways that were once unimaginable.

In the context of lunar and Martian habitats, cryptocurrency projects are being designed to address the unique challenges and opportunities of life beyond Earth. These digital currencies are expected to play a multifaceted role, serving not only as a medium of exchange but also as a cornerstone for the development of self-sustaining colonies.

One of the fundamental functions of these off-world cryptocurrencies is to enable the seamless exchange of goods and services within the colonies. From trading essential resources such as oxygen, water, and food to conducting inter-settlement commerce, these digital currencies will provide the necessary financial infrastructure to support the economic activities of lunar and Martian residents.

Moreover, these cryptocurrencies are expected to foster an environment of innovation and entrepreneurship in off-world settlements. As pioneers establish colonies and engage in a variety of enterprises, the digital currencies could facilitate investment, funding for research and development, and the emergence of new industries tailored to the unique conditions of space.

The development and utilization of cryptocurrency in lunar and Martian colonies also align with the spirit of decentralization and self-sufficiency. These digital currencies can provide a means of achieving economic independence from Earth, reducing reliance on traditional financial systems and intermediaries, and enabling a more resilient and sustainable financial ecosystem in the harsh and isolated environments of the Moon and Mars.

In essence, the exploration of cryptocurrency projects for lunar and Martian habitats represents a visionary step toward shaping the economic future of off-world settlements. These digital currencies are poised to play a pivotal role in establishing the financial infrastructure necessary for the success and sustainability of human presence beyond our home planet. As we prepare for this new era of space exploration, cryptocurrencies are at the forefront of forging the economic pathways that will define our future in the cosmos.

SPACE MINING AND TOKENIZATION:

The emerging industry of space mining is poised to transform the way we access valuable resources by tapping into the virtually limitless reserves of asteroids and celestial bodies. Within this burgeoning sector, a particularly innovative concept is gaining ground—cryptocurrency-based tokenization of space resources. This revolutionary approach seeks to tokenize the rights to mine and trade extraterrestrial resources, thereby introducing a novel form of financing for space mining ventures while establishing a tradable market in space resources.

Space mining is driven by the idea of extracting valuable materials, such as rare metals, water, and even fuel sources, from asteroids and other celestial bodies. These resources are not only valuable for use in space but also have significant potential for applications on Earth. However, space mining endeavors require substantial capital investment for the development of spacecraft, mining equipment, and the subsequent transportation of resources back to Earth or for use in space.

Cryptocurrency-based tokenization offers an innovative solution to the financial challenges of space mining. It involves creating digital tokens that represent ownership or access rights to space resources. These tokens can be bought, sold, and traded on cryptocurrency exchanges, providing a liquid and globally accessible market for space resource rights. This tokenization process allows space mining companies to raise capital by selling these tokens to investors who believe in the commercial potential of space mining.

Furthermore, tokenization introduces a level of democratization in space resource ownership. It enables individuals, not just institutional investors, to participate in the emerging space economy by purchasing tokens that grant them a stake in the future of space mining. This inclusivity opens up investment opportunities to a wider range of people, fostering a sense of community involvement in the space industry.

By establishing a tradable market for space resource rights through cryptocurrency-based tokenization, space mining companies can achieve several critical objectives. These include raising the necessary funds to fund ambitious missions, reducing the financial risks associated with space mining, and creating a dynamic, efficient, and accessible market for space resources. In doing so, they are setting the stage for a new era in space exploration, where the vast resources of the cosmos become not only accessible but also tradable commodities, transforming the way we envision the economic potential of space.

SPACE NFTs AND COLLECTIBLES:

The proliferation of Non-Fungible Tokens (NFTs) has transcended terrestrial boundaries, venturing into the realm of space exploration. This exciting development has given rise to a captivating niche within the NFT market – the creation of digital collectibles that represent space-related assets. These space-themed NFTs open up a new dimension of possibilities for space enthusiasts and collectors, offering a thrilling fusion of technology, art, and the cosmos.

Space-themed NFTs encompass a diverse range of digital collectibles, including but not limited to:

1. **Lunar Land Deeds:** NFTs representing virtual plots of lunar land. These digital deeds provide buyers with a virtual stake in lunar territory, catering to the age-old fascination of owning a piece of the Moon.

2. **Virtual Spacecraft Models:** NFTs that depict detailed, three-dimensional virtual models of iconic spacecraft, space stations, and rovers. These NFTs enable collectors to own and showcase intricate representations of humanity's achievements in space exploration.

3. **Astronomical Artwork:** NFTs featuring original art inspired by celestial bodies, space phenomena, and cosmic landscapes. These pieces of digital art not only serve as aesthetic expressions but also as a means of commemorating and celebrating our understanding of the cosmos.

4. **Space Missions Memorabilia:** NFTs that encapsulate the spirit and history of significant space missions. These digital collectibles may include mission patches, photographs, and commemorative items that evoke the rich legacy of space exploration.

The appeal of space-themed NFTs lies in their ability to merge the realms of technology and outer space. These digital collectibles offer collectors a unique opportunity to connect with humanity's space achievements in a tangible and interactive manner. Moreover, they cater to the innate curiosity and wonder associated with the cosmos, inviting enthusiasts to explore the universe from the comfort of their digital wallets.

As technology continues to advance and our understanding of space deepens, space-themed NFTs are likely to evolve, offering new and innovative collectibles that capture the excitement and beauty of the cosmos. This fusion of space exploration and blockchain technology not only adds an exhilarating facet to the NFT market but also commemorates humanity's relentless journey into the final frontier.

SPACE-BASED BLOCKCHAIN TECHNOLOGY:

The marriage of blockchain technology and space applications is a testament to the adaptability and versatility of blockchain beyond its traditional uses. In the context of space, blockchain's inherent characteristics of resilience, transparency, and security make it a valuable and indispensable tool for a myriad of space-related purposes.

One of the most prominent applications of blockchain in space endeavors is asset tracking. In the vast expanse of space, where assets can include spacecraft, satellites, rovers, and scientific instruments, ensuring the precise location and condition of these assets is paramount. Blockchain provides a tamper-proof and immutable ledger that can record the status and location of these space assets, ensuring their safety and proper management throughout their missions.

Securing communication in space is another pivotal application of blockchain technology. The vast distances between celestial bodies and spacecraft can introduce communication challenges, including the potential for data breaches or interference. Blockchain's cryptographic techniques enable the creation of secure and decentralized communication networks. These networks can safeguard sensitive data, secure interplanetary messaging, and protect against unauthorized access, ensuring that spacecraft can transmit and receive information securely and without interruption.

Furthermore, the integrity of space-based data is a critical concern in scientific research and space exploration. Blockchain can be utilized to record and authenticate data collected by space instruments, telescopes, and sensors. This data, once recorded on the blockchain, becomes verifiable and unchangeable, ensuring the reliability and authenticity of scientific findings.

Blockchain also plays a vital role in the development of decentralized and secure space systems. By employing blockchain-based solutions, space agencies and private companies can reduce the reliance on centralized systems, which can be vulnerable to single points of failure or security breaches. Instead, decentralized systems built on blockchain offer enhanced reliability and security, reducing the risks associated with critical space missions.

In sum, the intersection of blockchain technology and space applications represents a cutting-edge and forward-thinking approach to space exploration. Blockchain's resiliency, transparency, and security are leveraged to create a reliable infrastructure for asset tracking, secure communication, data integrity, and the development of decentralized space systems. As humanity continues to venture deeper into space, blockchain technology stands as an invaluable tool in ensuring the success and safety of these ambitious missions, ultimately contributing to our understanding of the cosmos.

CRYPTOCURRENCY FOR INTERSTELLAR TRAVEL:

The concept of interstellar travel represents the pinnacle of human exploration, pushing the boundaries of our understanding and capabilities. As we set our sights on the possibility of journeys beyond our solar system, one intriguing consideration is the role of cryptocurrencies in facilitating transactions that will be essential for the success of interstellar endeavors.

One of the fundamental challenges of interstellar travel is the vast distances that separate spacecraft, settlements, and potentially even extraterrestrial civilizations. The need for a financial system that can operate seamlessly across these cosmic expanses is evident. Traditional financial systems, with their reliance on centralized authorities and complex cross-border transactions, are ill-suited for the task. This is where cryptocurrencies step in as a compelling solution.

Cryptocurrencies possess several key attributes that make them highly suitable for interstellar transactions:

1. **Decentralization:** Cryptocurrencies operate without the need for central authorities or intermediaries. This means that transactions can occur directly between parties, regardless of their location in space. Interstellar travelers can send and receive digital currencies without the need for traditional banks or financial institutions.

2. **Borderless:** Cryptocurrencies transcend geographical and political boundaries. The same cryptocurrency can

be used on Earth, Mars, or on a spacecraft traveling between the stars. This borderless nature ensures that a single financial system can serve the entire interstellar community, providing a universal medium of exchange.

3. **Security:** The security features of cryptocurrencies, particularly their robust cryptographic techniques, provide protection against unauthorized access and fraudulent transactions. In the isolated and often harsh environment of space, the integrity and security of financial transactions become even more critical.

The use of cryptocurrencies in interstellar travel represents not only a practical solution to a complex challenge but also a visionary step toward preparing for a future where humanity engages with other civilizations beyond our solar system. As we explore the cosmos, the resilience, decentralization, and borderlessness of cryptocurrencies could play a pivotal role in fostering cooperation and commerce between distant space settlements, spacecraft, and potentially even with extraterrestrial entities. This forward-thinking approach aligns with the spirit of exploration and collaboration that defines our journey into the interstellar unknown.

SPACE CRYPTOCURRENCY REGULATION:

The regulatory landscape surrounding cryptocurrencies in space is a dynamic and evolving arena, mirroring the rapid growth of both the cryptocurrency and space exploration industries. As cryptocurrencies take on an increasingly integral role in funding and conducting transactions for space missions, it becomes imperative for space agencies, private space companies, and governments to adapt and establish a clear regulatory framework. This framework is vital not only to ensure compliance but also to address security concerns in the realm of space-based financial activities.

Several key aspects of the evolving regulatory framework for cryptocurrencies in space include:

1. **Space Commerce Regulations:** The development of regulations specific to space commerce is essential. These regulations encompass various activities, from space mining to the sale of space resources, where cryptocurrencies may be utilized for transactions. Such regulations will need to define the legal status of cryptocurrency transactions in space and address issues such as property rights and dispute resolution.

2. **Security and Compliance:** Regulations must emphasize the importance of security and compliance in space-based financial activities. Cryptocurrencies in space are not immune to risks such as fraud, theft, or illicit financial activities. Regulatory bodies need to establish security standards and compliance requirements to safeguard the integrity of space transactions.

3. **Cross-Border Transactions:** Space missions often involve collaborations between multiple countries and entities. The regulatory framework should consider the complexities of cross-border cryptocurrency transactions and the associated legal and tax implications.

4. **Digital Identities:** As cryptocurrency transactions in space are conducted by both humans and autonomous systems, the concept of digital identities and the management of private keys become crucial. Regulations may need to address issues of identity and access control for space-based cryptocurrency transactions.

5. **Interplanetary Regulations:** As we venture further into space and explore celestial bodies, including Mars and the Moon, regulations for cryptocurrency usage on different celestial bodies may need to be defined. These

regulations could address the unique challenges and opportunities associated with extraterrestrial financial activities.

6. **Global Collaboration:** The interconnected nature of space exploration and the international nature of cryptocurrencies necessitate global collaboration. International agreements and standards are essential to harmonize regulations and promote cooperation among spacefaring nations.

The dynamic nature of the cryptocurrency and space industries demands a proactive approach to regulation. Governments and regulatory bodies are increasingly recognizing the significance of cryptocurrencies in space activities and are working to develop appropriate rules and policies. Balancing innovation with compliance and security is a key challenge, and the regulatory framework for cryptocurrencies in space is expected to mature as the space industry expands and cryptocurrencies continue to gain prominence. This evolving regulatory framework is an essential component of ensuring the responsible and secure use of cryptocurrencies in the exciting realm of space exploration.

The intersection of cryptocurrency and space exploration represents an exciting frontier that showcases the adaptability and versatility of digital currencies in novel and challenging environments. As space exploration continues to advance, the role of cryptocurrencies is expected to expand, shaping the financial and economic landscape beyond Earth.

CRYPTOCURRENCY IN GAMING ECONOMIES

E xploring the intersection of cryptocurrencies and gaming economies is a fascinating subject that encompasses various sub-topics. To provide a comprehensive understanding, here are some sub-topics that can be covered:

IN-GAME CURRENCY AND CRYPTOCURRENCY:

The coexistence of cryptocurrencies and in-game currencies within virtual worlds represents a dynamic convergence of traditional gaming economics with the transformative potential of blockchain technology. In this symbiotic relationship, cryptocurrencies play a complementary role to in-game currencies, offering several distinct benefits for in-game transactions.

First and foremost, cryptocurrencies introduce a layer of versatility to the gaming ecosystem. While in-game currencies are typically confined to a specific game or platform, cryptocurrencies transcend these boundaries. Gamers can accumulate cryptocurrency holdings that extend beyond individual games, fostering a sense of digital ownership and investment. This versatility allows players to participate in various virtual economies, diversifying their assets and financial experiences.

Moreover, the integration of cryptocurrencies bolsters the concept of digital ownership in virtual worlds. Traditional in-game currencies lack the inherent rarity and transferability that cryptocurrencies offer through blockchain technology. Gamers can acquire unique digital assets or collectibles as non-fungible tokens (NFTs) and trade them across games and platforms, giving rise to a burgeoning market for virtual real estate, virtual items, and even entire virtual worlds. Cryptocurrencies provide the secure and transparent infrastructure needed for these cross-game transactions.

Another significant advantage lies in the potential for decentralization and player empowerment. Cryptocurrencies can facilitate player-driven economies, allowing gamers to influence the value of in-game assets and currency. Through blockchain-based governance models, players can collectively shape the rules and regulations governing their virtual realms. This democratization of virtual economies empowers players to have a say in the development and direction of the games they love.

The security and transparency inherent in cryptocurrencies offer a safeguard against fraud and illicit transactions in virtual worlds. Blockchain technology ensures that in-game transactions are recorded on an immutable ledger, reducing the risk of fraudulent activities. Additionally, smart contracts can be utilized to automate and enforce the terms of in-game transactions, adding an extra layer of security and trust for all participants.

Overall, the coexistence of cryptocurrencies and in-game currencies in virtual worlds opens up a new frontier for gamers and game developers alike. The benefits of using cryptocurrency for in-game transactions are evident in the form of digital ownership, versatility, security, and player empowerment. As this relationship continues to evolve, it holds the promise of transforming how we perceive and engage with virtual economies, offering players more control and a broader scope for financial engagement within the gaming universe.

OWNERSHIP OF IN-GAME ASSETS:

Blockchain technology and non-fungible tokens (NFTs) are catalyzing a profound revolution in the realm of digital asset ownership within the gaming industry. This transformation not only challenges traditional models of ownership but also introduces unprecedented benefits to gamers and developers alike.

At the core of this revolution is the concept of digital scarcity. In traditional gaming, digital assets, such as in-game items and skins, are generally non-scarce; they can be easily duplicated and have no inherent rarity. However, blockchain technology and NFTs introduce the notion of true digital ownership. Each NFT represents a unique, indivisible digital asset, and the ownership of these assets is recorded on a transparent and immutable blockchain ledger.

NFTs, as a cryptographic proof of ownership, bring authenticity and provenance to digital assets. This means that players truly own their in-game items, and these ownership records are tamper-proof and public, providing irrefutable evidence of ownership. It's a paradigm shift from the conventional notion of "renting" in-game items from game publishers.

The implications of this transformation are multifaceted. Gamers now have the ability to buy, sell, and trade their in-game assets with verifiable ownership records. The secondary market for in-game assets, powered by NFTs, has grown exponentially, providing gamers with new opportunities to monetize their gaming experiences. In some cases, players have earned significant incomes by trading rare or coveted in-game items as NFTs.

Furthermore, game developers benefit from this revolution by embracing player-driven economies. They can issue NFTs for in-game assets, enabling players to have true ownership. This shift fosters stronger player engagement, as gamers become stakeholders in the virtual economies, they participate in. Developers can also tap into the NFT market, selling unique in-game items as limited editions to generate revenue.

The integration of NFTs in gaming opens up the potential for cross-game interoperability, where assets can be used across multiple games or virtual worlds. Gamers can take their hard-earned NFT assets from one game to another, making their digital investments even more versatile and valuable.

In summary, blockchain technology and NFTs are reshaping the concept of digital asset ownership in games by introducing true scarcity, authenticity, and verifiable ownership. This transformation empowers gamers with new opportunities to monetize their gaming experiences and participate in player-driven economies. Game developers also benefit from this paradigm shift by creating stronger player engagement and revenue streams. The concept of true digital ownership within virtual worlds is rapidly becoming a reality, redefining how we perceive and interact with in-game assets.

DECENTRALISED GAMING PLATFORMS:

Blockchain-based gaming platforms represent a novel and disruptive approach to the gaming industry, offering decentralized experiences across various facets, from game development to publishing and distribution. This evolution challenges the traditional, centralized gaming model and ushers in a wave of innovation.

Game Development on Blockchain: Blockchain-based gaming platforms reimagine the development process. Game developers can utilize smart contracts to create blockchain-based games, enabling them to define unique in-game assets, establish rules, and govern the game's economy. This decentralized approach allows developers to have greater control over their creations, fostering creativity and reducing reliance on large game development studios.

Player Empowerment: One of the most significant shifts in blockchain-based gaming is the empowerment of players. Gamers can have a direct say in the development of games and the evolution of in-game economies through decentralized governance models. Their input can influence decisions related to updates, rules, and asset creation. This player-driven approach aligns more closely with the desires and interests of the gaming community.

Ownership and NFTs: Blockchain-based gaming platforms often incorporate non-fungible tokens (NFTs) to represent in-game assets. Players have true ownership of these assets, as their ownership is recorded on the blockchain. This means that gamers can buy, sell, or trade in-game items with verified ownership records, fostering a secondary market for these assets. NFTs revolutionize the concept of digital asset ownership within games, providing authenticity and verifiability.

Decentralized Publishing and Distribution: Blockchain technology enables decentralized publishing and distribution. Traditional game publishing and distribution models often involve a central authority controlling access to the game and its distribution. In contrast, blockchain-based platforms can use smart contracts to automate the publishing and distribution process, reducing intermediaries and making games more accessible to a global audience.

Cross-Platform Play: Blockchain-based gaming platforms are well-suited for cross-platform play, where gamers can use their in-game assets across multiple games and virtual worlds. The interoperability of assets across different games is facilitated by the underlying blockchain technology. This cross-game functionality adds a layer of versatility to the gaming experience, as players can leverage their assets in various contexts.

Monetization and Digital Economies: Blockchain-based gaming platforms introduce new monetization opportunities for gamers. Players can earn cryptocurrencies and other digital assets by participating in these decentralized gaming ecosystems. They can also engage in peer-to-peer trading of in-game items and assets. The gaming platform often provides a marketplace where these transactions can occur.

In conclusion, blockchain-based gaming platforms disrupt the traditional gaming industry by offering decentralized experiences in game development, publishing, and distribution. These platforms empower players, redefine digital asset ownership through NFTs, streamline publishing and distribution, enable cross-platform play, and introduce novel monetization options. The gaming community and developers are at the forefront of a revolution that places control, ownership, and creativity back in the hands of those who matter most—the players and creators.

CRPTOCURRENCY AND ESPORTS:

The impact of cryptocurrencies on the eSports industry is multifaceted and far-reaching, influencing various aspects such as player salaries, sponsorships, in-game prizes, and betting. This transformation is indicative of the broader trend of cryptocurrencies permeating the sports and entertainment landscape.

Player Salaries and Compensation: Cryptocurrencies are making inroads into how eSports players are compensated. While traditional payment methods remain prevalent, an increasing number of eSports organizations and players are exploring the option of receiving a portion of their salaries or bonuses in cryptocurrencies. This offers players greater financial flexibility and exposure to potential crypto asset appreciation.

Sponsorships and Brand Partnerships: Cryptocurrency companies have started to enter the eSports scene as sponsors and brand partners. These partnerships not only inject funds into the eSports ecosystem but also provide unique opportunities for players and organizations to engage with crypto-related products and services. Cryptocurrency brands may sponsor tournaments, teams, or individual players, broadening the financial horizons of eSports.

In-Game Prizes and Rewards: In some eSports games and platforms, cryptocurrencies are being used as in-game prizes and rewards. Players who excel in competitions may receive cryptocurrency-based rewards, adding a new layer of excitement to their victories. This approach can attract a broader audience and incentivize gamers to participate in eSports events.

Betting and Wagering: Cryptocurrencies are gaining prominence in eSports betting and wagering platforms. These platforms allow users to place bets on eSports events using cryptocurrencies, creating a seamless and decentralized betting experience. The advantage of cryptocurrencies in this context is the speed of transactions and the transparency of the blockchain, which ensures fairness and security in betting activities.

Fan Engagement and Crypto Tokens: Some eSports organizations and teams are issuing their own crypto tokens or fan tokens. These tokens can be used for various purposes, including voting on team decisions, accessing exclusive content, and participating in fan engagement activities. Crypto tokens deepen the connection between eSports entities and their fan base, offering a new way to interact and incentivize participation.

Financial Inclusion: Cryptocurrencies offer a degree of financial inclusion in eSports, especially for international players who may encounter challenges with traditional banking systems. Crypto payments provide a viable solution for cross-border payments and compensation, ensuring that eSports players worldwide can access their earnings efficiently.

Marketplace for Virtual Goods: In certain eSports games, players can earn or purchase virtual goods and assets, which they can then trade on cryptocurrency-based marketplaces. This secondary market for in-game items adds a new dimension to the eSports economy, enabling players to monetize their virtual achievements and investments.

The impact of cryptocurrencies on the eSports industry is still unfolding, with a growing number of players, organizations, and fans embracing the opportunities it presents. As the synergy between eSports and cryptocurrencies continues to evolve, it has the potential to reshape how the industry operates, from player compensation and sponsorships to fan engagement and in-game economies. This intersection of two dynamic and innovative fields promises an exciting future for eSports.

GAMING NFT MARKETPLACES:

NFT marketplaces dedicated to gaming assets have emerged as a dynamic and rapidly growing sector within the broader NFT ecosystem. These specialized platforms cater to the unique needs of gamers and virtual world enthusiasts, offering a marketplace for trading, buying, and selling in-game items, skins, characters, and even virtual real estate.

Decentraland Marketplace: Decentraland is a virtual world where users can create, explore, and monetize their content. The Decentraland Marketplace allows users to buy, sell, and trade virtual real estate and digital assets represented as

NFTs. This platform is particularly popular for its emphasis on virtual real estate, enabling users to purchase land parcels and develop their virtual creations.

CryptoKitties: CryptoKitties is a blockchain-based game where players collect, breed, and trade unique virtual cats. Each CryptoKitty is represented as an NFT, and the CryptoKitties Marketplace allows users to trade these digital felines. It was one of the earliest examples of NFT-based gaming and remains a prominent player in the space.

Rarible: Rarible is an NFT marketplace known for its flexibility and user-friendliness. While it supports various types of digital art and collectibles, it has gained traction for gaming-related NFTs. Users can create their own NFTs and trade them on the platform, making it a hub for independent artists, game developers, and gamers.

The Sandbox Marketplace: The Sandbox is a virtual gaming platform where users can create, own, and monetize their gaming experiences. The marketplace within The Sandbox enables the trade of LAND (virtual real estate) and ASSETS (in-game items, characters, and assets) as NFTs. It serves as a hub for the gaming community to exchange valuable in-game assets.

Axie Infinity Marketplace: Axie Infinity is a blockchain-based game where players collect, breed, and battle fantasy creatures called Axies. The Axie Infinity Marketplace allows players to trade Axies and their associated assets, which are NFTs. This game has gained significant popularity and boasts an active marketplace.

Immutable X: Immutable X is a Layer-2 scaling solution for Ethereum, designed to facilitate NFT trading for games. It offers gas-free and instant trades on the Ethereum network, making it a preferred choice for gamers and collectors. Various gaming projects have adopted Immutable X to host their in-game assets.

Enjin Marketplace: Enjin is a blockchain ecosystem for gaming, and its marketplace is dedicated to trading gaming assets as NFTs. Gamers can discover, purchase, and trade in-game items, including skins, characters, and other collectibles. Enjin's platform is known for its integration with various games and gaming communities.

These dedicated NFT marketplaces for gaming assets have created an ecosystem where gamers, developers, and collectors can interact and exchange their virtual possessions. The platforms empower users to truly own and trade their in-game items, adding a new dimension to the gaming experience. As the NFT and gaming industries continue to intersect, these marketplaces are likely to play an increasingly central role in the digital economies of virtual worlds.

GAMING COMMUNITIES AND CRYPTOCURRENCY:

Cryptocurrencies play a pivotal role in fostering gaming communities by offering a range of innovative tools and mechanisms that incentivize player participation and enable community-driven governance. These digital currencies have reshaped how gamers interact, collaborate, and contribute to the gaming ecosystem.

Incentivizing Player Participation: Cryptocurrencies provide a means to reward players for their participation and contributions to the gaming community. This can take the form of crypto-based incentives, such as tokens or in-game assets. Gamers are motivated to engage with the community, share knowledge, and actively participate in tournaments and events in exchange for these rewards. These incentives not only acknowledge and appreciate the efforts of players but also create a more dynamic and vibrant gaming community.

Player-Driven Economies: Cryptocurrencies have introduced player-driven economies within gaming communities. In these economies, players can buy, sell, and trade in-game items, assets, and collectibles represented as non-fungible tokens (NFTs). This not only empowers gamers to have true ownership of their in-game possessions but also fosters a sense of value and ownership within the community. Players are more likely to participate actively when they know that their efforts can translate into financial gains through cryptocurrency transactions.

Community Governance and Decision-Making: Cryptocurrencies enable decentralized and community-driven governance models within gaming platforms. Governance tokens are used to facilitate voting and decision-making processes. Gamers can have a say in the development of games, rules, and in-game economies. This level of player involvement ensures that gaming communities are aligned with the interests and preferences of their members. It also enhances transparency and trust within the community, as decisions are often made through consensus.

Support for Content Creators: Cryptocurrencies can be used to support content creators within gaming communities. Gamers can tip or donate cryptocurrencies to their favorite content creators or streamers as a form of appreciation for their content. This financial support not only encourages creators to produce more content but also creates a symbiotic relationship between content creators and their audience. This support can also help content creators sustain their careers and further enrich the gaming community.

Global Inclusivity: Cryptocurrencies break down geographical barriers and promote global inclusivity within gaming communities. Transactions and rewards are borderless, allowing gamers from different parts of the world to interact and collaborate. This global nature of cryptocurrencies creates a diverse and inclusive gaming community where players can engage with a wide range of individuals and cultures.

Deeper Community Engagement: Cryptocurrencies can facilitate deeper engagement within gaming communities through the use of blockchain technology. Gamers can trace the history and provenance of in-game assets and NFTs, ensuring trust and authenticity. This transparency fosters deeper connections and interactions within the community, as players can confidently trade, collaborate, and compete with one another.

In conclusion, cryptocurrencies are catalysts for building vibrant and engaging gaming communities. They incentivize player participation, enable community-driven governance, support content creators, promote global inclusivity, and facilitate deeper engagement. The integration of cryptocurrencies within gaming ecosystems adds a layer of excitement and potential for financial gain, contributing to the growth and dynamism of gaming communities.

CRYPTOCURRENCY-BASED GAMES:

Blockchain technology has given rise to a new genre of games known as "blockchain games" or "crypto games." These games are entirely built on blockchain technology and offer unique experiences and opportunities for players. Here are some examples of blockchain games:

1. *CryptoKitties:* CryptoKitties is one of the pioneering blockchain games that allows players to collect, breed, and trade virtual cats. Each CryptoKitty is a unique non-fungible token (NFT) on the Ethereum blockchain. Players can breed their CryptoKitties to create new and rare combinations, and each CryptoKitty has its own set of traits and attributes.

2. ***Axie Infinity:*** Axie Infinity is a blockchain-based game where players collect, breed, and battle fantasy creatures called Axies. Axies are NFTs, and players can earn cryptocurrency rewards by participating in battles and other in-game activities. The game has gained a large and active community of players.

3. ***Decentraland:*** Decentraland is a virtual world built on the Ethereum blockchain. It allows players to buy, sell, and develop virtual real estate represented as NFTs. In Decentraland, players can create and monetize content, socialize, and explore a virtual universe, with true ownership of their virtual land.

4. ***The Sandbox:*** The Sandbox is a blockchain-based gaming platform that enables players to create, own, and monetize their gaming experiences. Users can design and trade in-game assets and virtual real estate as NFTs. The platform also features a game maker tool that allows players to build their games.

5. ***My Crypto Heroes:*** My Crypto Heroes is a blockchain role-playing game (RPG) that combines historical characters and blockchain technology. Players collect and battle historical heroes, each represented as an NFT. The game incorporates elements of strategy and tactics.

6. ***Gods Unchained:*** Gods Unchained is a blockchain-based trading card game (TCG) that allows players to collect, trade, and battle with unique cards as NFTs. The game's cards are stored on the Ethereum blockchain, providing players with true ownership.

7. ***Crypto Space Commander (CSC):*** CSC is a space-based blockchain game that lets players own, customize, and command their spaceships. Players can trade spaceships and in-game assets as NFTs, and the game features a player-driven economy.

8. ***NBA Top Shot:*** While not a traditional game, NBA Top Shot is a blockchain-based platform that allows users to buy, sell, and trade officially licensed NBA collectible highlights as NFTs. It offers a unique way to engage with the world of sports.

These blockchain games offer players the opportunity to truly own in-game assets, engage in decentralized economies, and participate in a growing ecosystem of blockchain-based gaming. They provide a novel gaming experience that combines elements of entertainment, ownership, and the potential for financial gain through the trading of blockchain assets. As the technology continues to evolve, we can expect more innovative and immersive blockchain games to emerge in the future.

GAMING TOKENS AND ICOs:

Gaming tokens, Initial Coin Offerings (ICOs), and crowdfunding have become significant components of the gaming industry, shaping the way games are developed, funded, and monetized. Let's explore each of these aspects:

Gaming Tokens:

Gaming tokens, often referred to as utility tokens, are digital assets that have a specific use within a particular game or gaming platform. These tokens can be earned or purchased and are primarily used to access in-game items, characters, or features. Here are some key points regarding gaming tokens:

1. *In-Game Utility:* Gaming tokens are designed to offer in-game utility. Players can use these tokens to buy virtual goods, enhance their gaming experience, or access premium content within the game.

2. *Interoperability:* Some gaming tokens are built on blockchain technology, making them interoperable across multiple games and platforms. This means that a token earned or purchased in one game can potentially be used in another game within the same ecosystem.

3. *Economic Ecosystem:* Gaming tokens contribute to the creation of a self-contained economic ecosystem within a game. Players can buy, sell, and trade these tokens, often on secondary markets, adding a layer of real-world economic activity to the virtual gaming world.

Initial Coin Offerings (ICOs):

ICOs have been a popular method for game developers to raise funds for their projects. An ICO is a fundraising method where a new cryptocurrency or gaming token is sold to investors in exchange for funding. Here are some insights into ICOs in the gaming industry:

1. *Funding New Games:* Game developers use ICOs to raise capital for the development of new games or blockchain-based gaming platforms. Investors purchase the project's native tokens, which can later be used within the game.

2. *Investor Involvement:* ICO investors often receive tokens at a discounted rate during the ICO. These tokens can appreciate in value, and investors may become stakeholders in the success of the game or platform.

3. *Risks and Regulation:* ICOs in the gaming industry, as in other sectors, carry risks, including the potential for scams and regulatory challenges. It's important for

investors to conduct due diligence before participating in an ICO.

Crowdfunding in the Gaming Industry:

Crowdfunding has gained popularity as a means of financing gaming projects. Game developers can turn to crowdfunding platforms to raise funds directly from the gaming community. Here's how crowdfunding impacts the gaming industry:

1. ***Direct Support:*** Crowdfunding allows game developers to directly engage with their target audience and secure financial support from players who are excited about their project.

2. ***Transparency:*** Crowdfunding campaigns provide transparency into a game's development process. Backers can follow the project's progress and may even have the opportunity to provide feedback during development.

3. ***Reward-Based Crowdfunding:*** Many gaming-related crowdfunding campaigns offer backers rewards, such as early access to the game, exclusive in-game items, or other perks. This creates a sense of community involvement and rewards early supporters.

4. ***Platform Diversity:*** Crowdfunding can take place on various platforms, such as Kickstarter, Indiegogo, or even blockchain-based platforms. Each platform may have its own unique community and set of rules for campaigns.

In summary, gaming tokens, ICOs, and crowdfunding have all contributed to the evolution of the gaming industry by providing alternative methods of financing, engaging with the gaming community, and creating unique economic ecosystems within games. These mechanisms offer developers new ways to fund and monetize their projects while allowing players to have a more active role in shaping the gaming experiences they love. However, it's essential for both developers and investors to be aware of potential risks and regulatory considerations associated with these methods.

REGULATIONS AND SECURITY:

The use of cryptocurrencies in gaming brings forth various legal and security considerations that developers and players need to be aware of. These considerations encompass issues of fraud, hacking, and regulatory compliance. Let's delve into these key aspects:

1. Fraud Prevention:

Cryptocurrencies have introduced new avenues for fraud within the gaming industry. Here are some important points to consider:

- *Scams and Ponzi Schemes:* The gaming community can be susceptible to scams, such as fake ICOs or gaming token offerings. Players and investors should exercise caution and conduct thorough research before participating in any cryptocurrency-related gaming project.

- *Phishing Attacks:* Phishing attacks can trick gamers into revealing their private keys or wallet information. Developers should educate players about potential phishing risks and provide guidance on how to verify the authenticity of communication related to the game.

2. Hacking and Security:

The gaming industry has seen instances of hacking and security breaches related to cryptocurrencies. It's crucial to address these security concerns:

- *Wallet Security:* Players and developers should prioritize the security of cryptocurrency wallets. Implementing strong encryption, multi-factor authentication, and best practices for wallet management can help mitigate risks.

- *Smart Contract Vulnerabilities:* Games that utilize smart contracts on blockchain platforms should undergo rigorous security audits to identify and patch vulnerabilities. Vulnerable smart contracts can lead to substantial financial losses.

- *Exchanges and Marketplaces:* Many gaming tokens and assets are traded on cryptocurrency exchanges and marketplaces. These platforms are susceptible to hacking attempts, leading to the loss of funds. Players should choose reputable exchanges with a strong security track record.

3. Regulatory Compliance:

The use of cryptocurrencies in gaming often falls under the purview of regulatory authorities. Compliance with these regulations is essential:

- *Know Your Customer (KYC) and Anti-Money Laundering (AML) Requirements:* In some jurisdictions, gaming companies that deal with cryptocurrencies may be subject to KYC and AML regulations. This includes verifying the identities of users and reporting suspicious activities.

- ***Tax Implications:*** The tax treatment of in-game assets, cryptocurrency transactions, and the use of blockchain technology may vary by country. Developers and players should be aware of the tax regulations in their respective regions.

- ***Securities Laws:*** Some gaming tokens or assets could be classified as securities under certain regulations. Developers should seek legal advice to ensure compliance with securities laws when conducting ICOs or issuing gaming tokens.

- ***Licensing and Gambling Laws:*** Gaming platforms that use cryptocurrencies may be subject to licensing and gambling regulations in some jurisdictions. Compliance with these laws is critical to avoid legal complications.

In summary, the use of cryptocurrencies in gaming introduces a range of legal and security considerations. Players and developers must be vigilant against fraud, take measures to protect wallets and smart contracts, and ensure compliance with relevant regulatory requirements. Staying informed about the evolving regulatory landscape is crucial, as it may impact the use of cryptocurrencies in the gaming industry. By addressing these considerations, the gaming community can enjoy the benefits of cryptocurrencies while minimizing associated risks.

CRYPTOCURRENCY AND CROSS-PLATFORM GAMING:

Cryptocurrencies have the potential to revolutionize cross-platform transactions and interactions in the gaming world. They offer a decentralized and borderless means of exchanging value, making it easier for players to interact and trade assets across different gaming platforms. Here's how cryptocurrencies can facilitate cross-platform transactions and interactions in gaming:

Universal Currency: Cryptocurrencies can serve as a universal in-game currency that transcends individual gaming platforms. Players can acquire these cryptocurrencies in one game and use them in another, eliminating the need for separate in-game currencies. This simplifies cross-platform interactions by providing a common medium of exchange.

Interoperable Items: Some blockchain-based games and platforms create interoperable items as non-fungible tokens (NFTs). These items, such as skins, characters, or collectibles, can be moved seamlessly between compatible games or platforms. Cryptocurrencies can be used to purchase, trade, or upgrade these NFTs, allowing players to carry their assets across different gaming ecosystems.

Cross-Platform Marketplaces: Cryptocurrency-powered marketplaces enable players to trade in-game items and assets across platforms. These marketplaces act as intermediaries, facilitating secure peer-to-peer transactions. Cryptocurrencies, such as Ethereum or project-specific tokens, are used to conduct these trades, providing a unified currency for cross-platform transactions.

Decentralized Finance (DeFi) in Gaming: DeFi protocols built on blockchain networks allow players to lend, borrow, or earn interest on their gaming assets. Cryptocurrencies play a central role in these DeFi applications, providing liquidity and financial services for gamers. This financial infrastructure can be utilized across different games and platforms.

Global Tournaments and Competitions: Cryptocurrencies can be used to standardize prize pools and rewards in global gaming tournaments. Players from around the world can compete in cross-platform competitions, and the winnings can be distributed in cryptocurrency, ensuring fairness and ease of access for participants.

Innovative Gaming Experiences: Cryptocurrencies open the door to innovative gaming experiences that blend elements from multiple games. Developers can create metaverse-style environments where players can seamlessly transition between different gaming worlds, using a single cryptocurrency as the common currency for transactions.

Community-Driven Governance: Some blockchain games involve players in the decision-making process for the game's development and updates. Cryptocurrencies may be used to facilitate voting and governance, enabling players to have a say in the evolution of cross-platform gaming ecosystems.

Cross-Chain Solutions: To enhance interoperability, cross-chain solutions are being developed. These solutions aim to connect different blockchain networks, allowing assets and cryptocurrencies to move between chains. This technology can be instrumental in achieving cross-platform compatibility.

By leveraging cryptocurrencies, the gaming industry can break down barriers between gaming platforms, creating a more seamless and inclusive gaming experience. It promotes player autonomy, asset ownership, and cross-platform engagement, ultimately reshaping the way players interact and trade in the gaming world. As the technology continues to advance, we can expect even more innovative solutions to enhance cross-platform transactions and interactions.

VIRTUAL ECONOMIES AND REAL-WORLD IMPACT:

The success of in-game economies powered by cryptocurrencies has the potential to significantly influence real-world economics and investments. This analysis explores the key factors and implications of this influence:

1. Digital Asset Valuation: In-game assets, particularly those represented as NFTs, have real-world value driven by supply and demand dynamics. Players are willing to invest real money in acquiring these assets, and their value can appreciate over time. This creates a digital economy where the ownership and trading of virtual items can lead to substantial real-world profits. As these assets gain recognition and value, they can influence the broader understanding of digital asset valuation in the real world.

2. Investment Opportunities: The success of in-game economies has opened up new investment opportunities. Investors can participate in initial coin offerings (ICOs) or purchase gaming tokens associated with specific projects.

These tokens can appreciate in value based on the success of the underlying game or platform. The potential for significant returns has attracted the attention of both individual and institutional investors, creating a bridge between the gaming and investment worlds.

3. *Emerging Marketplaces:* Cryptocurrency-powered gaming marketplaces have created opportunities for entrepreneurs and developers to launch their own gaming projects. These projects can have a significant economic impact, as successful games can generate substantial revenue through token sales, in-game purchases, and trading fees. This entrepreneurial activity adds to the diversity of the cryptocurrency ecosystem and creates economic growth in both the gaming and blockchain sectors.

4. *Cross-Industry Collaboration:* The convergence of gaming and cryptocurrencies has led to cross-industry collaboration. Traditional financial institutions and blockchain companies are exploring partnerships with gaming platforms to offer financial services, including banking, lending, and investment products. This integration can expand the reach of cryptocurrency technologies into mainstream financial markets, influencing the broader economy.

5. *Skill Development and Employment:* The success of in-game economies has given rise to careers in blockchain development, game design, and digital asset management. This has led to skill development and employment opportunities in these emerging fields. The growth of in-game economies contributes to job creation and the development of a skilled workforce in the blockchain and gaming sectors.

6. *Taxation and Regulation:* As in-game economies gain prominence, tax authorities and regulators are paying closer attention to the income generated from cryptocurrency-based gaming activities. Taxation and regulatory frameworks are evolving to address the collection of taxes and ensure consumer protection. The success of these economies is influencing how taxation and regulation are applied to the cryptocurrency space.

7. *Real-World Economic Impact:* The success of in-game economies can have real-world economic consequences. As more individuals and businesses engage in cryptocurrency-related gaming activities, it contributes to the growth of the broader digital economy. This includes increased trading volume on cryptocurrency exchanges, the creation of new businesses, and the circulation of cryptocurrencies as a means of payment for goods and services.

In conclusion, the success of in-game economies powered by cryptocurrencies has a ripple effect on real-world economics and investments. It has redefined the valuation of digital assets, created new investment opportunities, facilitated cross-industry collaboration, generated employment, and impacted taxation and regulation. As these economies continue to grow, their influence on the broader economic landscape is likely to become more pronounced, shaping the future of both the gaming and cryptocurrency industries.

GAMING AND PLAY-TO-EARN:

The emergence of play-to-earn models in gaming represents a transformative shift in the gaming industry. These models allow players to earn cryptocurrency by participating in virtual worlds, creating a symbiotic relationship between gameplay and real-world rewards. Let's delve into the key aspects and implications of play-to-earn models:

1. Empowering Players: Play-to-earn models empower players by providing them with the opportunity to earn cryptocurrency through their in-game activities. This can include completing quests, achieving in-game milestones, or participating in various game-related tasks. Players are no longer just consumers; they become active contributors to the gaming ecosystem.

2. Tokenized In-Game Assets: In many play-to-earn games, in-game assets are tokenized as NFTs or fungible tokens. This means that the virtual items or currency earned within the game can have real-world value and can be traded or sold on cryptocurrency exchanges or within the game's marketplace. Players have ownership and control over these assets.

3. Economic Incentives: Play-to-earn models introduce strong economic incentives for players. They can earn cryptocurrency that can be used in other games, traded for real-world money, or held as an investment. This financial motivation can attract a broader audience to gaming and can lead to increased player engagement.

4. Financial Inclusion: Play-to-earn models have the potential to promote financial inclusion. Players from regions with limited access to traditional banking systems can participate and earn cryptocurrency, bridging the financial gap. This has the added benefit of expanding the global gaming community.

5. *Game Development Funding:* These models can provide sustainable funding for game development. Game creators can generate revenue by selling in-game assets, using blockchain-based mechanics. This revenue can be reinvested in the game's development and maintenance.

6. *Skill and Time Investment:* Earning cryptocurrency through play-to-earn models often requires a significant investment of time and skill. Players need to master the game and dedicate time to achieve rewards. This can be seen as a fair compensation model, where the more skilled and dedicated players earn more.

7. *Regulatory Considerations:* The intersection of cryptocurrencies, in-game assets, and play-to-earn models may raise regulatory questions. Authorities may scrutinize these models to determine whether they classify as gambling or financial services. The regulatory environment may evolve in response to this innovation.

8. *Market Growth:* Play-to-earn models are contributing to the growth of the blockchain gaming market. As more players enter these ecosystems, it fosters the creation of new games, platforms, and marketplaces that cater to this audience. The market is becoming increasingly diverse and competitive.

9. *Potential for Scams and Frauds:* The play-to-earn space is not without risks. Scammers may attempt to exploit players by promoting fraudulent games or schemes that promise earnings but result in losses. Players need to exercise caution and conduct due diligence before participating.

In summary, play-to-earn models in gaming are reshaping the relationship between players and virtual worlds. They offer financial incentives, create economic opportunities, and contribute to the growth of the blockchain gaming sector. However, they also introduce regulatory challenges and the need for player vigilance to protect against potential scams. As the gaming industry continues to evolve, play-to-earn models are likely to play a pivotal role in its future development.

GAMING TOKENS AND SMART CONTRACTS:

Smart contracts play a pivotal role in governing gaming ecosystems, offering a decentralized and automated framework for a wide range of functions. Here's an exploration of their role in gaming:

1. *Automated Payouts:* Smart contracts enable automated and instantaneous payouts to players based on predefined conditions. This is particularly valuable in competitive gaming, where rewards can be distributed automatically upon achieving specific milestones or winning tournaments. Players receive their earnings directly to their digital wallets, ensuring transparency and trust in the reward distribution process.

2. Non-Fungible Tokens (NFTs): In gaming, NFTs represent unique in-game assets such as characters, skins, and weapons. Smart contracts facilitate the creation and management of NFTs, ensuring the ownership and transfer of these assets. Players can buy, sell, or trade NFTs securely within the game ecosystem, and the ownership history is recorded on the blockchain, enhancing the provenance of virtual assets.

3. In-Game Marketplaces: Smart contracts power in-game marketplaces where players can trade virtual items, NFTs, or even cryptocurrencies. These contracts execute transactions and govern the exchange of assets, ensuring that all parties involved in a trade fulfill their obligations. This minimizes the risk of fraud and dispute, as the terms of the trade are automatically enforced.

4. Decentralized Governance: Gaming communities can use smart contracts to establish decentralized autonomous organizations (DAOs) that allow players to participate in the decision-making process. Through voting mechanisms coded in smart contracts, players can influence in-game changes, rules, and updates. This empowers the gaming community and ensures a more democratic approach to governance.

5. Anti-Cheating Mechanisms: Smart contracts can be designed to detect and prevent cheating in online games. They can enforce rules and fairness by verifying that players adhere to the game's code of conduct. Cheaters can be penalized automatically, providing a more secure and equitable gaming environment.

6. Player-Developed Content: In some blockchain-based gaming ecosystems, players have the ability to create and contribute to the game's content. Smart contracts enable content creators to be fairly compensated based on the popularity and usage of their creations. This fosters a collaborative and innovative gaming community.

7. Collectibles and Achievements: Smart contracts can be used to issue digital collectibles or achievements to players based on their in-game accomplishments. These collectibles can be unique and tradable, and their ownership can be verified through the blockchain.

8. *Transparent Rules and Code of Conduct:* Smart contracts can be designed to transparently articulate the rules and code of conduct within a game. This ensures that all players are aware of the rules and consequences for rule violations. The decentralized nature of smart contracts prevents unilateral rule changes by game developers, enhancing fairness.

9. *Interoperability:* In some instances, smart contracts enable interoperability between different games and platforms. Players can use their in-game assets or achievements across multiple games, creating a seamless and unified gaming experience.

In conclusion, smart contracts are integral to the governance of gaming ecosystems. They automate payouts, manage NFTs, power in-game marketplaces, and enforce rules. Their transparent and decentralized nature ensures trust and fairness within the gaming community. As the gaming industry continues to evolve, smart contracts will play an increasingly significant role in shaping the future of gaming.

SECURITY TOKENS IN GAMING:

Security tokens have gained prominence as a means to represent ownership in gaming companies and projects, offering a unique approach to fundraising and investment in the gaming industry. Let's delve into the key aspects of security tokens and their utilization in gaming:

1. Funding Mechanism: Security tokens are employed as a fundraising mechanism for gaming companies and projects. These tokens are typically backed by real-world assets, revenue-sharing agreements, equity, or other financial instruments related to the gaming venture. Investors acquire security tokens as a form of ownership in the company or project.

2. Investment Opportunities: Security tokens create investment opportunities for both traditional and crypto-savvy investors. Individuals and institutions can invest in gaming companies and projects without the traditional barriers to entry. This expands the pool of potential investors and fosters a more diverse and global investor base.

3. Equity Ownership: In the gaming industry, security tokens can represent equity ownership in a gaming company. Investors holding these tokens have a stake in the company's profits, losses, and decision-making processes. This allows for a more direct and tangible form of ownership, similar to traditional equity shares.

4. Revenue Sharing: Some security tokens entitle their holders to a share of the gaming company's revenue. This innovative model aligns the interests of investors with the success of the gaming project. Investors can benefit from the project's financial performance, making security tokens an attractive investment option.

5. Governance and Decision-Making: Security tokens may also grant voting rights to their holders, allowing them to participate in the governance and decision-making processes of the gaming company or project. Investors have a say in strategic directions, game development choices, and other key decisions.

6. Liquidity and Trading: Security tokens are often traded on regulated security token exchanges. This provides liquidity to investors, enabling them to buy and sell their ownership stakes in gaming companies and projects. The presence of secondary markets enhances the appeal of security tokens.

7. Regulatory Compliance: Security tokens are typically subject to regulatory oversight, depending on the jurisdiction in which they are issued. Gaming companies and projects that issue security tokens must comply with securities regulations, providing investors with legal protections.

8. *Tokenization of Gaming Assets:* Beyond ownership in companies, security tokens can also represent ownership in gaming assets, such as virtual real estate or rare in-game items. This tokenization of gaming assets allows players and investors to participate in the virtual economy with real-world ownership rights.

9. *Mitigation of Risks:* Security tokens aim to mitigate risks associated with traditional fundraising methods. By offering a digital and regulated framework for ownership, they reduce the potential for fraud, enhance transparency, and provide investors with clear legal rights.

In summary, security tokens are an innovative and regulated way to represent ownership in gaming companies and projects. They offer investment opportunities, equity ownership, revenue-sharing arrangements, and governance rights. Their presence in the gaming industry has the potential to democratize investment and foster a more diverse and engaged gaming community. However, regulatory compliance is essential, as security tokens are subject to legal oversight in many jurisdictions.

THE FUTURE OF CRYPTOCURRENCY:

The relationship between cryptocurrency and gaming is poised to continue evolving in the coming years, presenting various speculations and predictions for this dynamic intersection:

1. Increased Integration of Cryptocurrencies in In-Game Economies: We can expect a deeper integration of cryptocurrencies within in-game economies. More games will adopt blockchain-based tokens or cryptocurrencies for in-game purchases, trading, and rewards. This integration will provide players with greater control and ownership of their digital assets.

2. Play-to-Earn Models Becoming the Norm: Play-to-earn models, where players can earn cryptocurrencies by participating in games, are likely to become increasingly prevalent. Gamers will be incentivized to invest time and skill in virtual worlds, potentially making gaming a source of income for many.

3. NFTs Expanding Beyond Collectibles: Non-fungible tokens (NFTs) will expand beyond collectibles and art to represent a broader range of in-game assets. Items like weapons, skins, and unique characters will become tokenized, allowing players to truly own and trade these assets within and across games.

4. *Blockchain Gaming Platforms:* Blockchain-based gaming platforms will grow, offering decentralized experiences for game development, publishing, and distribution. These platforms will empower independent developers, reduce the influence of major gaming corporations, and foster a more diverse gaming ecosystem.

5. *Enhanced Gaming Communities:* Cryptocurrencies will continue to play a crucial role in fostering gaming communities. They will incentivize player participation, governance, and content creation. Gamers will be rewarded with tokens for contributing to the community, driving engagement and collaboration.

6. *Cross-Platform Interoperability:* The gaming industry will move closer to achieving cross-platform interoperability. Cryptocurrencies will facilitate seamless transactions and asset transfers between different games and gaming platforms, providing players with more flexibility and freedom.

7. *eSports and Cryptocurrency Integration:* eSports will further embrace cryptocurrencies, with players and teams receiving salaries, sponsorships, and prizes in digital currencies. Betting on eSports events using cryptocurrencies will also continue to rise, adding another layer of engagement and excitement.

8. Regulatory Clarity: As the relationship between cryptocurrency and gaming deepens, regulatory bodies are likely to establish clearer guidelines and regulations. This will provide a more secure environment for investors, players, and developers and reduce uncertainties.

9. Gaming Tokens and Crowdfunding: Gaming tokens, initial coin offerings (ICOs), and crowdfunding will continue to be popular methods for financing gaming projects. These avenues will allow developers to raise capital and involve the gaming community in project development.

10. The Metaverse and Virtual Reality (VR): The metaverse, a collective virtual shared space, and VR gaming will become more intertwined with cryptocurrencies. Virtual spaces will offer opportunities for ownership, trade, and social interaction, creating entirely new gaming experiences.

11. Cryptocurrency-Backed Games: Games will emerge that are entirely built on blockchain technology, offering unique and innovative gaming experiences. These games will leverage the security and transparency of blockchain while pushing the boundaries of creativity.

12. Gaming and Real-World Economies: The success of in-game economies powered by cryptocurrencies will have a growing impact on real-world economics and investments. Virtual assets will gain economic significance, leading to new investment opportunities and a deeper connection between digital and physical economies.

13. Decentralized Governance in Gaming: Decentralized autonomous organizations (DAOs) will play a more prominent role in gaming, allowing players to actively participate in decision-making processes, rule changes, and game development.

14. Enhanced Gaming Security: Cryptocurrencies will bring improved security to gaming, reducing the risk of fraud, hacking, and cheating through transparent and immutable transaction records.

In conclusion, the relationship between cryptocurrency and gaming is expected to undergo significant transformations in the coming years. The integration of cryptocurrencies, NFTs, and blockchain technology will redefine the gaming experience, making it more player-centric, immersive, and economically significant. These developments will likely reshape the gaming industry and influence how we play, engage, and interact in virtual worlds.

QUANTUM COMPUTING AND CRYPTOCURRENCY SECURITY

The convergence of quantum computing and cryptocurrency security is a multifaceted domain encompassing quantum computing fundamental, cryptographic underpinnings, emerging quantum threats, and quantum-resistant solutions. Quantum computers, with their unique computational capabilities, pose a potential risk to the cryptographic algorithms that safeguard cryptocurrencies. This quantum threat has prompted the development of quantum-resistant cryptography, seeking to fortify the security of digital assets in a post-quantum era. As quantum technology advances, the cryptocurrency community is diligently preparing for this quantum challenge, exploring quantum-resistant cryptographic methods, regulatory considerations, and quantum key distribution, all while contemplating the future landscape of cryptocurrency security in a quantum world.

QUANTUM COMPUTING BASICS:

Quantum computing, a paradigm-shifting field at the intersection of physics and computer science, introduces a revolutionary approach to information processing. Unlike classical computers, which rely on bits as the fundamental unit of data, quantum computers leverage quantum bits, or qubits, to harness the fascinating principles of quantum mechanics. These principles include superposition, entanglement, and quantum interference. Superposition allows qubits to exist in multiple states simultaneously, exponentially increasing computational power. Entanglement enables qubits to be intimately connected regardless of the physical distance between them, providing a unique mode of information transfer. Quantum interference allows quantum computers to exploit destructive and constructive interference to perform specific calculations with remarkable efficiency. This introduction lays the foundation for understanding how quantum computing challenges classical cryptographic methods, influencing the security of cryptocurrencies and prompting the search for quantum-resistant cryptographic solutions.

Quantum bits, or qubits, represent a quantum leap in computing capabilities due to their extraordinary properties, fundamentally different from classical bits. Qubits can exist in a state of superposition, allowing them to represent both 0 and 1 simultaneously. This enables quantum computers to process vast amounts of information in parallel, exponentially increasing their computational power as more qubits are employed. Furthermore, qubits exhibit entanglement, a phenomenon where the state of one qubit is intrinsically linked to the state of another, even when separated by vast distances. This property allows for the creation of highly correlated qubit pairs, which is essential for quantum cryptography and secure communication. Quantum interference, another unique property of qubits, enables quantum computers to perform certain calculations much more efficiently than classical computers. These properties, superposition, entanglement, and interference, underpin the superior computational power of quantum computers and their potential to disrupt classical cryptographic methods, including those used in cryptocurrency security.

Quantum algorithms represent a groundbreaking area of quantum computing, offering the potential to solve complex mathematical problems at unprecedented speeds when compared to classical computers. Several notable quantum algorithms have emerged, each tailored to tackle specific mathematical challenges. Shor's algorithm, for instance, stands out for its capacity to factor large numbers exponentially faster than classical algorithms. This property poses a significant threat to widely-used cryptographic methods such as RSA encryption, which relies on the difficulty of factoring large numbers. Grover's algorithm, on the other hand, excels at unstructured search problems and can potentially offer quadratic speedup over classical algorithms. Quantum algorithms like these have the potential to compromise the security of classical cryptographic systems and demand the development of quantum-resistant cryptographic techniques, including those employed in cryptocurrency security.

CRYPTOGRAPHIC FUNDAMENTALS:

Cryptographic techniques are the bedrock of security within blockchain and cryptocurrency systems. Public-key cryptography plays a pivotal role in ensuring the integrity and confidentiality of transactions. In this system, each user has a pair of cryptographic keys: a public key for encryption and a private key for decryption and digital signature generation. Transactions are secured by combining these keys and cryptographic functions, making it computationally infeasible to derive the private key from the public key, ensuring secure ownership and transaction verification. Hash functions are another essential cryptographic tool employed in blockchain. They convert data, such as transaction details or blocks, into fixed-length strings of characters, creating a digital fingerprint. This fingerprint, or hash, is used to verify data integrity and is essential for creating the structure of blockchain's immutable and secure ledger. Together, these cryptographic techniques establish trust and security in cryptocurrency transactions and blockchain networks.

Encryption plays a paramount role in securing cryptocurrency transactions and wallets. It ensures the confidentiality and integrity of sensitive data in these decentralized systems. When a user initiates a cryptocurrency transaction, the transaction details are encrypted, transforming them into unreadable ciphertext. This encryption prevents unauthorized parties from intercepting and deciphering transaction information during transit. In addition, cryptocurrency wallets, which store users' public and private keys, are often protected by encryption. The private key, which is the key to accessing and managing one's digital assets, is encrypted and should only be decrypted with the wallet's password or authentication method. This dual-layer of encryption safeguards the private key, making it extremely difficult for malicious actors to gain unauthorized access to a user's cryptocurrency holdings. In essence, encryption is the cornerstone of cryptocurrency security, ensuring that transactions and digital assets remain confidential and tamper-resistant.

Public-key cryptography and digital signatures are fundamental components of blockchain technology, ensuring the security and authenticity of transactions and data within the decentralized ledger. In this cryptographic system, each participant in the blockchain network possesses a pair of cryptographic keys: a public key and a private key.

Public Key: The public key is shared openly and is associated with a user's wallet address. It is used to encrypt data, such as transaction details or messages, intended for the owner of the corresponding private key.

Private Key: The private key is kept confidential and is used for decrypting data encrypted with the corresponding public key. It is also employed to create digital signatures.

Digital Signatures: When a user initiates a transaction within the blockchain, they use their private key to generate a digital signature. This signature is a cryptographic proof of the transaction's authenticity and the user's identity. It ensures that the transaction has not been tampered with during transmission.

The digital signature, the transaction data, and the public key of the sender are all bundled together and stored in the blockchain. Anyone with access to the blockchain can verify the transaction's authenticity by using the public key associated with the sender's wallet address to decrypt the signature. If the decrypted signature matches the original transaction data, the transaction is considered valid and secure.

Public-key cryptography and digital signatures are pivotal for enabling trust and security in blockchain technology. They validate the origin and integrity of transactions, ensuring that data within the blockchain remains immutable and resistant to fraud or manipulation.

THREATS POSED BY QUANTUM COMPUTING:

Shor's Algorithm: Shor's algorithm, developed by mathematician Peter Shor, is a quantum algorithm that has profound implications for cryptocurrency security. This algorithm is designed to efficiently factor large composite numbers into their prime components, which is a problem that classical computers struggle with when the numbers are extremely large. The security of widely-used cryptographic methods, such as RSA encryption, relies on the difficulty of factoring large numbers.

In the context of cryptocurrency security, Shor's algorithm poses a significant threat to the widely adopted public-key cryptography systems. Many cryptocurrencies use

164

cryptographic algorithms based on the difficulty of factoring large semiprime numbers to secure transactions and wallets. If Shor's algorithm were to become practical on large-scale quantum computers, it could potentially break these cryptographic systems, compromising the security of cryptocurrencies.

Grover's Algorithm: Grover's algorithm, formulated by Lov Grover, is another quantum algorithm with implications for cryptocurrency security. Unlike Shor's algorithm, Grover's algorithm does not threaten encryption directly but targets search problems. It is designed to search unsorted databases quadratically faster than classical algorithms.

In cryptocurrency security, Grover's algorithm could potentially impact hashing functions used in blockchain systems. While it does not break encryption directly, it could theoretically reduce the time required to find a hash collision or reverse hash functions. This might weaken some aspects of blockchain security, such as the immutability of transaction blocks.

To counter these quantum threats, researchers are actively exploring and developing quantum-resistant cryptographic methods that can withstand the computational power of quantum computers. These post-quantum cryptography techniques aim to ensure the continued security of cryptocurrencies in a world where quantum computers may become a reality.

In summary, Shor's algorithm threatens the security of cryptocurrency systems that rely on factoring large numbers, while Grover's algorithm could impact the efficiency of hashing functions in blockchain networks. The development and adoption of quantum-resistant cryptographic solutions are crucial to maintaining the security of cryptocurrencies in the face of quantum computing advancements. How quantum computers can potentially break widely-used cryptographic algorithms.

The timeline for the development of quantum computers capable of breaking current cryptographic standards is still uncertain, but several factors influence the expectations for their development:

Quantum Computing Progress: The development of quantum computers has been advancing steadily, with major technology companies, research institutions, and governments investing in quantum research. Quantum hardware has been improving in terms of qubit stability and coherence times. However, large-scale, fault-tolerant quantum computers that can tackle complex cryptographic problems are not yet a reality.

Quantum Supremacy: In October 2019, Google claimed to have achieved quantum supremacy, demonstrating a quantum computer's ability to solve a specific problem faster than the most advanced classical supercomputers. While this was a significant milestone, the problem solved was not related to cryptography, and it does not signify immediate quantum threats to current cryptographic standards.

NIST's Post-Quantum Cryptography Initiative: The U.S. National Institute of Standards and Technology (NIST) has been actively working on standardizing post-quantum cryptographic algorithms. This initiative aims to prepare cryptographic methods that can withstand quantum attacks when large-scale quantum computers become available. Several promising quantum-resistant cryptographic techniques are being considered.

Quantum-Resistant Cryptography Research: Cryptographers and researchers are proactively working on quantum-resistant cryptographic algorithms and methods. While these approaches may not be as efficient as current cryptographic standards, they are designed to provide security even in the face of quantum threats.

Commercial Quantum Computing Ventures: Private companies like IBM, Google, and startups such as Rigetti are actively exploring quantum computing. They are offering access to cloud-based quantum computers, fostering research and experimentation in the field.

Expectations vary, but it is generally believed that large-scale quantum computers capable of breaking current cryptographic standards are at least a decade or more away. Nevertheless, the timeline is highly dependent on technological advancements and breakthroughs in quantum hardware and software. As a result, the development of quantum-resistant cryptographic standards and their adoption in cryptocurrency and blockchain systems is gaining momentum to ensure security in a post-quantum world.

QUANTUM-RESISTANT CRYPTOGRAPHY:

Quantum-resistant cryptographic algorithms are a critical response to the potential threat that quantum computers pose to classical cryptographic systems. As quantum computers have the potential to break widely used encryption methods, quantum-resistant algorithms are designed to withstand quantum attacks, ensuring the continued security of digital communications and transactions.

These cryptographic algorithms rely on mathematical problems that are believed to be difficult for both classical and quantum computers to solve. Unlike classical encryption, which relies on the factorization of large numbers (as seen in RSA encryption) or the discrete logarithm problem (as in ECC), quantum-resistant cryptography employs mathematical constructs that remain secure in a quantum computing environment.

Common quantum-resistant cryptographic algorithms include:

1. *Lattice-based Cryptography:* These algorithms rely on the hardness of lattice problems, making them resistant to Shor's algorithm, which is designed to factor large numbers efficiently. Lattice-based schemes include NTRUEncrypt and Ring-LWE.

2. *Hash-Based Cryptography:* These algorithms leverage the security of cryptographic hash functions to create digital signatures and other cryptographic primitives. One well-known example is the Merkle Signature Scheme (MSS).

3. ***Multivariate Polynomial Cryptography:*** These schemes involve the challenge of solving systems of multivariate polynomial equations, which are computationally hard for both classical and quantum computers. The Unbalanced Oil and Vinegar (UOV) scheme is an example of this category.

4. ***Code-Based Cryptography:*** These algorithms rely on the complexity of decoding linear error-correcting codes. The McEliece cryptosystem is a famous example, known for its resistance to quantum attacks.

5. ***Isogeny-Based Cryptography:*** Isogeny-based schemes use the mathematics of elliptic curves and the difficulty of computing isogenies between them. SIKE (Supersingular Isogeny Key Encapsulation) is one such example.

These quantum-resistant cryptographic algorithms offer a layer of security against the potential advent of powerful quantum computers. While they may not be as efficient as classical cryptographic methods, they provide a vital defense against quantum attacks. As the development of quantum-resistant cryptography progresses, these algorithms are being considered for integration into various digital systems, including cryptocurrencies, to ensure robust security in a quantum-empowered future.

Post-quantum cryptography schemes, designed to resist attacks from quantum computers, encompass a variety of mathematical constructs and algorithms. Here are examples of post-quantum cryptographic schemes:

1. **Lattice-Based Cryptography:**

   NTRUEncrypt: A lattice-based encryption scheme, NTRUEncrypt relies on the hardness of the NTRU problem, which involves finding short lattice vectors. It is considered one of the leading candidates for post-quantum secure encryption.

2. **Hash-Based Cryptography:**

   Merkle Signature Scheme (MSS): MSS is a one-time signature scheme based on cryptographic hash functions. It is considered a practical and secure option for post-quantum digital signatures.

3. **Code-Based Cryptography:**

   McEliece Cryptosystem: McEliece is a well-established code-based cryptosystem that relies on the difficulty of decoding linear error-correcting codes. It is among the earliest candidates for post-quantum secure encryption.

4. **Multivariate Polynomial Cryptography:**

   Unbalanced Oil and Vinegar (UOV): UOV is a multivariate polynomial-based signature scheme that poses a hard problem for quantum and classical computers alike. It is a contender in the post-quantum cryptography landscape.

5. **Isogeny-Based Cryptography:**

Supersingular Isogeny Key Encapsulation (SIKE): SIKE relies on the mathematics of isogenies between supersingular elliptic curves. It is considered a leading candidate for post-quantum key exchange.

6. **Code-Based Cryptography:**

BIKE (Bit-flipping Key Encapsulation): BIKE is a code-based key exchange protocol that is designed to be secure against quantum attacks. It aims to provide a practical and efficient post-quantum solution.

7. **Hash-Based Cryptography:**

XMSS (eXtended Merkle Signature Scheme): XMSS is a stateful hash-based digital signature scheme that provides long-term security against both classical and quantum adversaries.

8. **Lattice-Based Cryptography:**

FrodoKEM: FrodoKEM is a lattice-based key exchange mechanism that is designed for post-quantum security. It offers a balance between security and efficiency.

9. **Multivariate Polynomial Cryptography:**

Rainbow: Rainbow is a multivariate polynomial-based digital signature scheme that is known for its resistance to quantum attacks.

10. Isogeny-Based Cryptography:

SIKE: Apart from key exchange, SIKE (Supersingular Isogeny Key Encapsulation) also includes a digital signature scheme, offering a versatile post-quantum solution.

These post-quantum cryptography schemes are actively being studied and evaluated by the cryptographic community to ensure they provide robust security in a world where quantum computers could potentially threaten classical cryptographic systems.

The cryptocurrency community recognizes the need to transition to quantum-resistant standards to safeguard digital assets and ensure the long-term security of blockchain networks. Efforts in this direction involve several key aspects:

1. *Research and Development:* Cryptocurrency developers and researchers are actively investigating quantum-resistant cryptographic algorithms. They aim to identify and implement post-quantum cryptographic solutions

that can replace existing standards when quantum computers become a threat.

2. ***Standards and Protocols:*** Organizations and standards bodies within the cryptocurrency space are actively working on defining and adopting quantum-resistant cryptographic standards. This includes the development of new public-key algorithms, digital signatures, and encryption methods that can withstand quantum attacks.

3. ***Forks and Updates:*** Cryptocurrency projects may undergo hard forks or software updates to integrate quantum-resistant standards. This transition is often gradual and planned well in advance to ensure a smooth migration for the entire blockchain network.

4. ***Quantum-Safe Wallets:*** Wallet providers are developing quantum-safe wallets that utilize post-quantum cryptographic techniques. These wallets are designed to protect users' private keys and transactions from quantum attacks.

5. ***Community Education:*** Cryptocurrency communities are actively educating users about the importance of quantum resistance and the need to migrate to quantum-safe standards when the time comes. This includes creating awareness about the potential threats posed by

quantum computers and the steps users should take to protect their digital assets.

6. ***Partnerships and Collaborations:*** Cryptocurrency projects often collaborate with research institutions and cryptographic experts to develop and evaluate quantum-resistant solutions. These partnerships aim to accelerate the adoption of quantum-safe standards within the cryptocurrency space.

7. ***Quantum-Resistant Testnets:*** Some blockchain projects create testnets to experiment with quantum-resistant algorithms and assess their performance and security. These testnets help validate the feasibility of transitioning to quantum-resistant standards.

8. ***Security Audits:*** Cryptocurrency projects conduct security audits to assess the robustness of quantum-resistant solutions. These audits involve thorough testing and evaluation to identify and address vulnerabilities.

9. ***User Preparation:*** Cryptocurrency users are encouraged to prepare for the quantum threat by migrating to quantum-resistant wallets and standards when they become available. This proactive approach helps protect users' assets against potential quantum attacks.

The transition to quantum-resistant standards within the cryptocurrency community is a proactive response to the evolving landscape of quantum computing. While quantum computers capable of breaking current cryptographic standards may still be years away, the community is taking steps today to ensure the security and longevity of blockchain networks and digital assets in a post-quantum era.

THE IMPACT ON BITCOIN AND OTHER CRYPTOCURRENCIES:

The vulnerability of cryptocurrencies like Bitcoin to quantum attacks is a topic of growing concern within the crypto community and among researchers. Quantum computing has the potential to disrupt the security mechanisms that underpin many of the world's most widely used encryption algorithms, including those used in cryptocurrencies. Here are some key points to consider:

1. *Current Encryption Standards:* The security of cryptocurrencies relies on various cryptographic techniques, particularly public-key cryptography, such as the elliptic curve digital signature algorithm (ECDSA) for Bitcoin. These encryption methods are currently considered secure against classical computers but are vulnerable to attacks from powerful quantum computers.

2. ***Shor's Algorithm:*** Shor's algorithm, developed by Peter Shor in 1994, is one of the most well-known quantum algorithms with the potential to break widely used encryption schemes. It can factor large numbers exponentially faster than the best-known classical algorithms, which is a critical threat to the security of cryptocurrencies.

3. ***Quantum Computers' Progress:*** Quantum computing technology is advancing, and researchers are making progress in building more powerful quantum computers. While large-scale, fault-tolerant quantum computers are not yet available, it is widely believed that they could become a reality in the coming decades.

4. ***Quantum-Resistant Cryptography:*** To mitigate the risk of quantum attacks, some cryptocurrencies and blockchain projects are exploring or implementing quantum-resistant cryptographic algorithms. These algorithms are designed to be secure against both classical and quantum computers. Examples include lattice-based cryptography, hash-based cryptography, and code-based cryptography.

5. ***Transition Period:*** Implementing quantum-resistant cryptography in existing blockchain networks is challenging, as it would require a hard fork or significant

changes to the underlying technology. This transition period could introduce security vulnerabilities and requires careful planning.

6. ***Quantum-Secure Upgrades:*** Some cryptocurrency projects are proactively working on upgrading their systems to be quantum-secure, but many others have not yet addressed this issue. It is crucial for the crypto community to adopt quantum-resistant standards before large-scale quantum computers become a reality.

7. ***Quantum Threat Timeline:*** The timeline for when quantum computers will become a practical threat to cryptocurrencies is uncertain. It depends on the rate of progress in quantum computing technology, but estimates vary from a decade or more to several decades.

8. ***Quantum Key Distribution (QKD):*** Quantum key distribution is an emerging technology that uses the principles of quantum mechanics to secure communication. While QKD has potential applications in securing cryptocurrency transactions, it also faces technical and practical challenges for widespread adoption.

In conclusion, the vulnerability of cryptocurrencies like Bitcoin to quantum attacks is a real concern. As quantum computing technology advances, it becomes increasingly important for the cryptocurrency community to address these potential threats. Whether through the adoption of quantum-resistant cryptography, the development of quantum-secure upgrades, or the integration of quantum key distribution, the industry must remain vigilant to ensure the long-term security of blockchain networks in a post-quantum world.

The security and integrity of blockchain networks could face several potential consequences due to various factors, including technological advancements, malicious actors, and external events. Here are some key considerations:

1. *Quantum Attacks:* As mentioned in the previous response, quantum computing poses a significant threat to the security of blockchain networks. If large-scale quantum computers become available, they could potentially break the encryption used in many blockchain networks, compromising the security and privacy of transactions. This could lead to unauthorized access and theft of funds.

2. *Double-Spending Attacks:* Blockchain networks rely on consensus mechanisms to validate and secure transactions. If an attacker gains control over the majority of a blockchain's computing power (a 51%

attack), they can potentially double-spend coins or manipulate the blockchain's transaction history, undermining its integrity.

3. *Smart Contract Vulnerabilities:* Smart contracts are self-executing contracts with the terms of the agreement directly written into code. Vulnerabilities in smart contracts can lead to financial losses and security breaches. Malicious actors can exploit code flaws, leading to hacks and loss of funds.

4. *Malware and Phishing:* Malware and phishing attacks can compromise the security of users' private keys or credentials. If attackers gain access to private keys, they can steal cryptocurrencies. Blockchain networks themselves may not be directly affected, but users' security is compromised.

5. *Centralization Risks:* Some blockchain networks face centralization risks due to a concentration of mining power, governance, or ownership of tokens. Centralization can lead to censorship, collusion, or manipulation of network rules, which can undermine the integrity and security of the blockchain.

6. *Network Forks and Upgrades:* While hard forks and network upgrades are essential for the evolution of blockchain networks, they can introduce vulnerabilities

and security risks. Contentious hard forks can lead to chain splits, causing confusion and potential security issues for users.

7. ***Regulatory and Legal Challenges:*** Blockchain networks may face legal and regulatory challenges that impact their security and integrity. Regulatory crackdowns, legal disputes, and changes in legal frameworks can lead to instability and uncertainty within the ecosystem.

8. ***Lack of Adoption and Network Fragmentation:*** If blockchain networks fail to achieve widespread adoption and network effects, they may become less secure due to reduced computational power securing the network. Smaller networks are more susceptible to attacks and lack the integrity and security of larger, established networks.

9. ***Smart Contract Complexity:*** Complex smart contracts can be difficult to audit thoroughly, increasing the risk of undiscovered vulnerabilities and potential exploits. The security of blockchain networks is closely tied to the security of the code running on them.

10. ***Environmental Concerns:*** Proof-of-Work (PoW) blockchains, like Bitcoin, face security and environmental concerns due to the energy consumption

associated with mining. Environmental concerns could lead to pressure on PoW blockchains to transition to more sustainable consensus mechanisms, potentially impacting network security.

In summary, blockchain networks are not immune to various security and integrity challenges. The blockchain industry must continually adapt and evolve to address these potential consequences, with a focus on improving the security of the technology, mitigating risks, and adhering to best practices to ensure the long-term viability and trust in these systems.

The cryptocurrency community is taking various steps to prepare for the quantum threat and to ensure the security and longevity of blockchain networks in a post-quantum world. Here are some of the measures being taken:

1. ***Research and Development:*** Cryptocurrency projects and blockchain developers are actively researching and developing quantum-resistant cryptographic algorithms. These algorithms aim to be secure against both classical and quantum computers. Examples of such algorithms include lattice-based cryptography, hash-based cryptography, and code-based cryptography.

2. ***Protocol Upgrades:*** Some cryptocurrency projects have already started implementing quantum-resistant

cryptography in their protocols. This involves making changes to the underlying blockchain technology and algorithms, which often requires a hard fork. These upgrades aim to protect existing transactions and wallets from future quantum attacks.

3. *Quantum-Secure Wallets:* Hardware and software wallet providers are working on quantum-secure wallet solutions. These wallets use quantum-resistant cryptographic techniques to protect users' private keys and transactions from quantum attacks.

4. *Quantum Key Distribution (QKD):* Some cryptocurrency projects are exploring the use of quantum key distribution (QKD) to enhance security. QKD uses the principles of quantum mechanics to secure communications by providing a theoretically unbreakable way to exchange encryption keys. This can be particularly relevant for securing transactions and communications on blockchain networks.

5. *Education and Awareness:* The cryptocurrency community is making efforts to educate users and stakeholders about the potential quantum threat. Promoting awareness about the need for quantum-resistant measures and secure practices is essential to protect users from future vulnerabilities.

6. ***Collaboration with Research Community:*** Cryptocurrency projects are collaborating with academic researchers and institutions specializing in post-quantum cryptography. This collaboration helps ensure that the cryptographic solutions adopted are thoroughly vetted and secure.

7. ***Regular Security Audits:*** Blockchain networks, especially those with smart contracts, undergo regular security audits to identify and rectify vulnerabilities. These audits are essential to maintain the security and integrity of the blockchain, especially in the face of emerging threats like quantum attacks.

8. ***Testing and Simulation:*** Some projects are simulating quantum attacks to assess the vulnerability of their systems and to develop countermeasures. This testing helps identify potential weaknesses and allows for proactive solutions.

9. ***Standards and Best Practices:*** The industry is working on establishing quantum-resistant standards and best practices to guide blockchain developers and network operators in protecting their systems against quantum threats.

It's important to note that the quantum threat to cryptocurrencies is still in the future, and the timeline for the development of practical quantum computers remains uncertain. Nonetheless, the proactive steps taken by the cryptocurrency community demonstrate a commitment to staying ahead of potential threats and ensuring the long-term security of blockchain networks. As quantum computing technology evolves, these preparations will become increasingly vital for the continued success of the cryptocurrency ecosystem.

QUANTUM-SAFE SOLUTIONS:

Quantum-safe solutions in the context of cryptocurrency are cryptographic techniques and strategies that aim to protect blockchain networks and digital assets from the potential threats posed by quantum computing. As quantum computers advance, their ability to break existing encryption methods used in cryptocurrencies may compromise the security and integrity of blockchain transactions. Here are some quantum-safe solutions being explored in the cryptocurrency space:

1. *Quantum-Resistant Cryptography:* Cryptographers are developing and implementing quantum-resistant cryptographic algorithms that are believed to be secure against both classical and quantum computers. These

algorithms are designed to withstand quantum attacks like Shor's algorithm, which can factor large numbers exponentially faster than classical computers. Examples include lattice-based cryptography, hash-based cryptography, and code-based cryptography.

2. *Post-Quantum Signatures:* Quantum-resistant signature schemes are being developed to replace existing cryptographic signatures like the elliptic curve digital signature algorithm (ECDSA). These signatures ensure the authenticity of transactions and protect them from quantum attacks. One example is the "Lamport Signature."

3. *Quantum-Safe Wallets:* Hardware and software wallet providers are working on quantum-safe wallet solutions. These wallets use quantum-resistant cryptographic techniques to secure users' private keys and transactions, ensuring they remain protected even in a quantum computing environment.

4. *Quantum Key Distribution (QKD):* Some cryptocurrency projects are exploring the use of quantum key distribution to enhance security. QKD uses the principles of quantum mechanics to secure the exchange of encryption keys, providing a theoretically

unbreakable way to protect communications and transactions on blockchain networks.

5. ***Hash Function Upgrades:*** Cryptographic hash functions are fundamental to blockchain security. Quantum-safe hash functions are being considered to replace existing ones. Algorithms like SHA-256, used in Bitcoin, may be vulnerable to quantum attacks, and transitioning to quantum-safe hashes is an important step.

6. ***Standardization and Best Practices:*** The cryptocurrency community is working on establishing standards and best practices for quantum-safe solutions. These guidelines help ensure that developers and network operators implement the right security measures to protect their systems from quantum threats.

7. ***Preparedness and Contingency Planning:*** Cryptocurrency projects are taking steps to prepare for the quantum threat. This includes contingency planning for potential hard forks and upgrades to implement quantum-resistant cryptography. Early planning is crucial to avoid security vulnerabilities during the transition.

8. ***Research and Development:*** Ongoing research in post-quantum cryptography is essential for staying ahead of

quantum threats. Cryptographers and developers are continuously working to improve and adapt quantum-safe solutions as quantum computing technology advances.

It's important to note that the timeline for the development of practical quantum computers remains uncertain. However, the cryptocurrency community is taking a proactive approach to ensure the long-term security and integrity of blockchain networks. The adoption of quantum-safe solutions will be critical in safeguarding digital assets and the trust in cryptocurrencies as quantum computing technology evolves.

The development and implementation of quantum-resistant cryptographic techniques are essential to protect digital assets and secure communication in a post-quantum computing world. Here's how these techniques are being developed and integrated into the field of cryptography:

1. *Algorithm Development:* Cryptographers are actively researching and designing new cryptographic algorithms that are believed to be resistant to quantum attacks. These algorithms are designed to replace or augment existing cryptographic standards to ensure long-term security.

Prominent examples of quantum-resistant algorithms include lattice-based cryptography, hash-based cryptography, code-based cryptography, and multivariate polynomial cryptography.

2. *NIST Post-Quantum Cryptography Standardization:* The National Institute of Standards and Technology (NIST) in the United States has been leading the effort to standardize post-quantum cryptographic algorithms. NIST initiated a multi-year process to evaluate and select quantum-resistant algorithms that could be adopted as industry standards.

NIST's effort involves soliciting and evaluating candidate algorithms, with the goal of creating a set of quantum-resistant standards for various cryptographic purposes, including encryption, digital signatures, and key exchange.

3. *Open-Source Implementations:*

Many quantum-resistant cryptographic algorithms are being implemented as open-source software libraries. This encourages collaboration, peer review, and widespread adoption.

Cryptographers and developers can access and integrate these libraries into various software applications and systems, including blockchain networks and cryptocurrency wallets.

4. ***Testing and Evaluation:*** Cryptographers subject quantum-resistant algorithms to extensive testing and evaluation to assess their security, performance, and practicality. This includes testing for resistance against known quantum attacks and other vulnerabilities.

   Rigorous security assessments are crucial to gain confidence in the strength of these algorithms.

5. ***Education and Adoption:*** Educational efforts are vital to raise awareness of the need for quantum-resistant cryptography and to ensure that developers and organizations understand the implications of quantum computing on existing cryptographic methods.

   Industry organizations, academic institutions, and cryptographic experts are actively promoting the adoption of quantum-resistant techniques and best practices.

6. ***Migration Strategies:*** As quantum-resistant algorithms are developed and adopted, there is a need for migration

strategies to transition existing systems to these new cryptographic standards. This can be a complex process and may involve hard forks or significant changes to cryptographic infrastructure.

7. ***Quantum Key Distribution (QKD):*** Quantum key distribution (QKD) is another approach to securing communications against quantum threats. It leverages the principles of quantum mechanics to enable the exchange of encryption keys securely. QKD is considered to be theoretically unbreakable even by quantum computers.

8. ***Interoperability and Compatibility:*** Compatibility between existing cryptographic infrastructure and quantum-resistant techniques is a consideration during implementation. Ensuring a smooth transition and avoiding disruption is important for maintaining the security of systems.

9. ***Continued Research:*** Cryptographic research is an ongoing process. As quantum computing technology evolves, researchers will continue to explore and develop new cryptographic techniques that adapt to emerging threats and challenges.

The development and implementation of quantum-resistant cryptographic techniques are critical for safeguarding the security and integrity of digital assets, as well as for ensuring the long-term viability of encryption methods in a world where quantum computers pose a significant threat to classical cryptographic systems.

Upgrading existing blockchain networks to withstand quantum attacks is a complex and crucial task. It involves transitioning to quantum-resistant cryptographic techniques and making changes to the network's architecture. Here are some strategies for upgrading existing blockchain networks to be quantum-resistant:

1. *Quantum-Resistant Cryptography:* Replace existing cryptographic algorithms with quantum-resistant alternatives. Some examples include lattice-based cryptography, hash-based cryptography, and code-based cryptography. This transition typically requires a hard fork, a network upgrade that is not backward-compatible with the old rules.

2. *Gradual Transition:* Plan for a gradual transition to quantum-resistant cryptography. Allow users to migrate their existing addresses and funds to the new format, ensuring a smooth and non-disruptive process.

3. *Multi-Algorithm Support:* Support multiple cryptographic algorithms simultaneously to

accommodate both classical and quantum-resistant cryptography. This can be achieved by creating hybrid addresses that use both types of algorithms.

4. *Post-Quantum Signatures:* Implement post-quantum digital signatures for transaction validation and authentication. This helps protect transactions against quantum threats.

5. *Monitoring and Auditing:* Regularly monitor the network for potential vulnerabilities and security risks. Conduct security audits to identify and rectify any issues, especially related to the implementation of quantum-resistant techniques.

6. *Community Education:* Educate the blockchain community about the transition to quantum-resistant cryptography, its importance, and the steps users need to take to secure their assets in the new paradigm.

7. *Developer Collaboration:* Collaborate with the development community to ensure that blockchain software clients and wallets are updated to support quantum-resistant cryptographic standards.

8. *Secure Key Management:* Emphasize secure key management practices. Encourage users to upgrade to quantum-safe wallets that protect their private keys against quantum attacks.

9. ***Communication Channels:*** Use secure communication channels for important announcements and upgrades to avoid phishing attacks that exploit users during the transition period.

10. ***Quantum Key Distribution (QKD):*** Consider implementing quantum key distribution for enhanced security. QKD can be used to secure communication channels between network nodes and users.

11. ***Testing and Simulations:*** Simulate quantum attacks to assess the network's vulnerability to quantum threats and fine-tune the quantum-resistant measures in place.

12. ***Contingency Planning:*** Prepare for potential challenges and contingencies that may arise during the transition, such as network forks, contentious community debates, and technical difficulties.

13. ***Collaboration with Research Community:*** Work with academic institutions and researchers specializing in post-quantum cryptography to ensure the security of the chosen cryptographic standards.

14. ***Governance and Decision-Making:*** Ensure transparent governance and decision-making processes within the blockchain community to build consensus on the need for quantum-resistant upgrades and the choice of cryptographic standards.

15. ***Regulatory Considerations:*** Stay informed about regulatory changes and ensure compliance with evolving legal requirements as they pertain to blockchain technology.

16. ***Economic Incentives:*** Consider economic incentives, such as rewards or incentives for miners or stakers who upgrade their infrastructure and adopt quantum-resistant standards. This can help incentivize network security.

Upgrading an existing blockchain network to withstand quantum attacks is a complex and multifaceted process that requires careful planning, collaboration, and education. It's important to address this issue proactively to ensure the long-term security and integrity of the blockchain ecosystem as quantum computing technology advances.

THE ROLE OF QUANTUM KEY DISTRIBUTION:

Quantum Key Distribution (QKD) is a quantum-secure encryption method that leverages the principles of quantum mechanics to provide an exceptionally high level of security for transmitting encryption keys. QKD is designed to offer a level of security that is theoretically unbreakable, even by powerful quantum computers. Here's an overview of QKD and its key features:

1. *Quantum Mechanics:* QKD is based on the principles of quantum mechanics, a branch of physics that describes the behavior of particles at the quantum level. Quantum mechanics introduces unique properties, such as superposition and entanglement, that form the basis of QKD's security.

2. *Key Distribution:* The primary purpose of QKD is to securely distribute cryptographic keys between two parties, traditionally referred to as Alice and Bob. These keys can be used for secure communication through classical encryption methods like symmetric-key cryptography.

3. *Unpredictability:* In QKD, the security of key distribution relies on the fundamental unpredictability of quantum states. Quantum particles, such as photons, exhibit properties that cannot be predicted with certainty. For example, the polarization of a single photon can be in multiple states simultaneously, a property known as superposition.

4. *Quantum Entanglement:* QKD often employs quantum entanglement, a phenomenon where the properties of two or more particles become correlated even when they are physically separated. Any changes made to one entangled particle will instantaneously affect the other, regardless of

the distance between them. This property allows QKD to detect any interception or eavesdropping attempts.

5. *Detection of Eavesdropping:* QKD is designed to detect any attempt by a third party (Eve) to intercept the quantum keys during transmission. When an eavesdropping attempt occurs, it disturbs the quantum states, and this disturbance can be detected by Alice and Bob. This enables them to discard compromised keys and initiate a new key exchange.

6. *Secure Key Generation:* After detecting any eavesdropping, Alice and Bob can use the remaining uncompromised quantum keys to generate secure shared encryption keys. Since they are aware of the eavesdropping attempt, they can choose to repeat the key exchange process until they are confident in the security of the keys.

7. *Information-Theoretic Security:* The security of QKD is often described as "information-theoretically secure." This means that the security of the system is based on the fundamental laws of physics and is not dependent on computational assumptions. It provides security against both classical and quantum attacks.

8. *Practical Challenges:* While QKD offers high security, it comes with practical challenges. Quantum key distribution systems require specialized equipment, such as single-photon sources, detectors, and secure transmission channels. These systems can be complex and expensive to implement.

9. Commercial Deployments: Despite the challenges, QKD has been deployed in some critical applications, including secure communication for government and financial institutions. It is used to protect highly sensitive data where the highest level of security is essential.

10. Ongoing Research: Research in QKD continues to advance, aiming to make the technology more practical, cost-effective, and accessible for a broader range of applications.

In summary, Quantum Key Distribution (QKD) is a quantum-secure encryption method that exploits the fundamental properties of quantum mechanics to achieve an extremely high level of security in key distribution. It offers the promise of truly secure communications even in a world with powerful quantum computers. However, it is important to note that QKD is still an evolving technology with practical challenges that need to be addressed for broader adoption.

Quantum Key Distribution (QKD) has the potential to enhance the security of cryptocurrency transactions by providing a fundamentally secure method for key exchange and encryption. Here's how QKD can contribute to the security of cryptocurrency transactions:

1. *Unbreakable Encryption Keys:* QKD generates encryption keys that are theoretically unbreakable, even by quantum computers. This ensures that the private keys used in cryptocurrency transactions are highly resistant to quantum attacks. As quantum computers advance, the security of classical cryptographic methods may be compromised, but QKD remains secure.

2. *Protection against Quantum Attacks:* Cryptocurrencies rely on public-key cryptography, such as elliptic curve digital signatures (ECDSA), to secure transactions. Quantum computers could potentially break these encryption methods using algorithms like Shor's algorithm. QKD provides a quantum-secure way to exchange keys, protecting the confidentiality and integrity of transactions.

3. *Eavesdropping Detection:* QKD includes mechanisms for detecting eavesdropping attempts during key exchange. If an attacker tries to intercept the quantum key exchange, this interference will be detectable, and the compromised keys can be discarded. This ensures that transaction data remains confidential.

4. ***Secure End-to-End Communication:*** QKD can be used to secure communication channels between cryptocurrency users, nodes, and wallets. By employing QKD, the parties can establish secure communication, which is crucial for protecting private keys, wallet addresses, and transaction information.

5. ***Protection of Wallets and Private Keys:*** Cryptocurrency wallets store private keys, which are the most critical components for accessing and managing digital assets. QKD can enhance the security of wallet management by providing secure channels for key exchange and preventing eavesdropping attempts.

6. ***Securing Network Nodes:*** Cryptocurrency networks rely on nodes to validate and relay transactions. Implementing QKD in the communication between nodes enhances the overall security of the network and prevents potential threats from malicious nodes or eavesdroppers.

7. ***Improved Security for Exchanges:*** Cryptocurrency exchanges, which hold large volumes of digital assets, can benefit from QKD to protect their cold storage solutions, hot wallets, and communication between trading partners. This added layer of security can reduce the risk of theft and hacking incidents.

8. ***Resistance to Future Threats:*** As quantum computing technology progresses, it is essential to prepare for the potential quantum threats that cryptocurrencies may face. Integrating QKD into cryptocurrency networks and services provides a proactive defense against future threats.

9. ***Long-Term Security:*** Cryptocurrency networks are designed to be secure over the long term, and quantum computing poses a potential long-term threat. Integrating QKD into the infrastructure helps ensure the security of digital assets and transactions for years to come.

It's important to note that implementing QKD in cryptocurrency networks requires significant technological and infrastructural changes. Additionally, QKD technology is still evolving, and there are practical challenges to its widespread adoption. Nevertheless, it offers a promising solution for enhancing the security of cryptocurrency transactions, particularly in the face of the growing quantum threat. As quantum technology matures, the integration of QKD into the cryptocurrency ecosystem may become increasingly important to maintain the security and trust of digital assets.

Implementing Quantum Key Distribution (QKD) for cryptocurrencies comes with several practical challenges and considerations that need to be addressed to ensure a successful integration. Here are some of the key challenges and considerations:

1. *Infrastructure and Equipment Costs:* QKD systems require specialized hardware, including single-photon sources, detectors, and secure transmission channels. These components can be expensive, making the initial investment a significant challenge for widespread adoption.

2. *Quantum Network Architecture:* Building a secure quantum network infrastructure, especially on a global scale, is a complex task. Developing quantum repeaters to extend the range of QKD, creating secure communication links, and ensuring network compatibility are considerable challenges.

3. *Key Distribution Speed:* QKD systems typically generate keys at a much slower rate compared to classical key exchange methods. This can be a practical limitation when high-speed transactions are essential in cryptocurrency networks.

4. *Interoperability:* Ensuring that QKD systems are compatible with existing cryptocurrency network

protocols and standards can be challenging. Smooth integration requires careful planning and cooperation between quantum and cryptocurrency experts.

5. *Security of Endpoints:* The security of the endpoints, such as cryptocurrency wallets and nodes, must be maintained. If an attacker compromises these endpoints, it can undermine the security provided by QKD. Protecting endpoints is a crucial part of the overall security strategy.

6. *Key Management:* Proper key management is essential. Cryptocurrency users and entities must securely store and manage their QKD-generated keys. Loss or compromise of these keys can lead to significant security risks.

7. *Network Upgrades:* Introducing QKD to an existing cryptocurrency network may necessitate network upgrades or hard forks. Coordinating these upgrades and ensuring smooth transitions can be challenging.

8. *Regulatory and Legal Compliance:* Cryptocurrency projects implementing QKD must consider the regulatory and legal implications of this technology.

Compliance with evolving laws and regulations is essential.

9. ***Educational Challenges:*** Users and network operators must understand the significance of QKD and how to use it properly. Educating the cryptocurrency community about the advantages, best practices, and potential limitations of QKD is crucial.

10. ***Quantum Attacks:*** While QKD provides a strong level of security against quantum attacks, it is not immune to all potential threats. As quantum technology advances, new attack vectors may emerge, and QKD systems may require updates to address these evolving threats.

11. ***Scalability:*** Ensuring that QKD solutions are scalable to handle large volumes of transactions and network traffic is an important consideration for cryptocurrencies with a high level of activity.

12. ***Standardization:*** The standardization of QKD and its integration with cryptocurrency protocols can be challenging. Cryptographic standards and consensus mechanisms for QKD need to be established.

13. ***Economic Feasibility:*** The economic feasibility of implementing QKD, considering the associated costs, potential energy consumption, and the value it brings to the cryptocurrency network, is a key consideration.

While QKD holds great promise for enhancing the security of cryptocurrencies in a post-quantum world, these practical challenges and considerations need to be carefully addressed to ensure a successful and effective integration. Collaboration between quantum experts, cryptocurrency developers, and relevant stakeholders is essential to navigate these challenges and drive the adoption of QKD in the cryptocurrency space.

QUANTUM COMPUTING AND BLOCKAIN CONSENSUS:

Quantum computing has the potential to significantly impact consensus algorithms like Proof of Work (PoW) and Proof of Stake (PoS), which are fundamental to blockchain networks. Here's an examination of how quantum computing may affect these consensus algorithms:

1. Impact on Proof of Work (PoW):

Mining Vulnerability: Quantum computers, with their ability to perform complex calculations exponentially faster than classical computers, could threaten the security of PoW-based blockchains. PoW relies on miners solving cryptographic puzzles to validate transactions and add blocks to the blockchain. A sufficiently powerful quantum computer could potentially solve these puzzles much faster than traditional miners, giving them an unfair advantage in the network.

Centralization Risks: If quantum computers become a practical threat to PoW networks, there may be a rush for miners to adopt quantum technology to maintain a competitive edge. This could lead to a centralization of mining power, as those with access to quantum computing capabilities may dominate the network.

Upgrade Challenges: Transitioning from PoW to a quantum-resistant consensus algorithm is not a simple task. It would require a hard fork and extensive changes to the network's infrastructure. Planning for this transition and achieving consensus within the community can be challenging.

Energy Consumption: PoW blockchains are known for their energy-intensive mining process. Quantum computing might exacerbate these energy concerns if quantum miners were to compete with traditional miners in solving cryptographic puzzles.

2. Impact on Proof of Stake (PoS):

Key Vulnerability: PoS blockchains rely on validators (often referred to as "stakers") who hold a certain amount of the native cryptocurrency to propose and validate new blocks. These validators use private keys to sign transactions and participate in the network. Quantum computers could potentially break the private keys, compromising the security of the network.

Mitigation through Quantum-Resistant Cryptography: PoS networks can mitigate quantum threats by adopting quantum-resistant cryptographic algorithms. By replacing traditional digital signatures with quantum-resistant ones, the networks can protect the private keys of stakers against quantum attacks.

Wallet Security: The security of stakers' wallets and their private keys is of utmost importance. Stakers must use quantum-resistant wallets to ensure their private keys remain secure, even in a quantum computing environment.

Continued Research: PoS blockchains need to stay informed about the development of quantum computing technology and the latest quantum-resistant cryptographic standards. Ongoing research is essential to adapt to evolving threats.

Overall Impact on Both PoW and PoS:

1. Quantum computing may accelerate the need for a transition to quantum-resistant cryptographic standards and consensus algorithms. Blockchain projects need to proactively address these concerns to ensure the long-term security of their networks.

2. The transition to quantum-resistant solutions will require collaboration within the blockchain community and cooperation between quantum experts and blockchain developers.

3. Quantum-resistant solutions, such as quantum-resistant cryptographic algorithms, quantum key distribution, and post-quantum cryptography, will play a critical role in protecting the integrity of blockchain networks against the quantum threat.

In summary, quantum computing has the potential to impact both PoW and PoS consensus algorithms by introducing vulnerabilities and security risks. However, with careful planning, adoption of quantum-resistant solutions, and ongoing research, blockchain networks can prepare for the quantum threat and ensure the continued security of their transactions and digital assets.

Maintaining the security and integrity of blockchain networks in a post-quantum era requires proactive strategies and careful planning. Here are some key approaches and considerations:

Adopt Quantum-Resistant Cryptography:

Transition to quantum-resistant cryptographic algorithms to protect transactions and data from quantum attacks. Examples include lattice-based cryptography, hash-based cryptography, and code-based cryptography.

Standardization and Best Practices:

Work towards the establishment of quantum-resistant cryptographic standards and best practices for blockchain networks. Collaboration with industry organizations and cryptographic experts is crucial in this effort.

Continuous Monitoring and Auditing:

Regularly monitor the network for potential vulnerabilities and conduct security audits to identify and address any issues, especially those related to quantum-resistant solutions.

Key Management:

Emphasize secure key management practices, including the use of quantum-resistant wallets and hardware security modules (HSMs) for storing and managing private keys.

Quantum Key Distribution (QKD):

Consider implementing quantum key distribution for enhanced security in communication between network nodes and users.

Economic Incentives:

Provide economic incentives for miners, stakers, and validators who upgrade their infrastructure to support quantum-resistant standards. This can encourage the adoption of secure practices.

Security Awareness and Education:

Educate users, developers, and network operators about the quantum threat and the importance of adopting quantum-resistant solutions and best practices.

Flexible Upgrade Path:

Plan for a flexible upgrade path to transition existing systems to quantum-resistant standards. This may involve hard forks or significant changes to the network.

Research and Collaboration:

Collaborate with academic institutions, cryptographic researchers, and experts in post-quantum cryptography to stay informed about the latest developments and ensure the security of the chosen cryptographic standards.

Secure Endpoints:

Ensure that endpoints, such as wallets and network nodes, are secure and regularly updated. The compromise of endpoints can undermine the security of the network.

Regulatory Compliance:

Stay informed about regulatory changes and ensure compliance with evolving legal requirements as they relate to blockchain technology and quantum-resistant solutions.

Quantum-Safe Testing and Simulation:

Conduct quantum-resistant testing and simulations to assess the network's vulnerability to quantum threats and fine-tune the quantum-resistant measures in place.

Scalability:

Ensure that quantum-resistant solutions are scalable to handle large volumes of transactions and network traffic, particularly for cryptocurrencies with high activity.

Quantum Computing Progress Monitoring:

Continuously monitor the development of quantum computing technology and assess the timeline for when large-scale quantum computers might become practical threats.

Network Diversity:

Consider diversifying the network by adopting hybrid consensus mechanisms or multiple cryptographic standards to reduce the risk associated with a single point of failure.

Emergency Response Plans:

Develop contingency plans to respond to potential quantum threats and network disruptions. These plans should include communication strategies and emergency upgrades.

In a post-quantum era, blockchain networks need to adapt to the evolving threat landscape by implementing quantum-resistant solutions, collaborating with experts, and maintaining a proactive stance towards security. By adopting a holistic approach that addresses cryptographic, technical, economic, and educational aspects, blockchain networks can continue to offer secure and reliable transactions and data storage.

REGULATORY AND POLICY CONSIDERATIONS:

Government and industry efforts to address the quantum threat to cryptocurrency are essential to ensure the security and integrity of digital assets in the face of advancing quantum computing technology. Here's an overview of the initiatives and strategies in place:

1. Government Initiatives:

a. Research Funding: Many governments are investing in quantum research to better understand quantum computing and its potential impact on various sectors, including finance and cryptography.

b. Regulatory Frameworks: Governments are considering or developing regulatory frameworks to address the use of quantum-resistant encryption in financial systems and digital assets. This includes measures to ensure that cryptocurrencies comply with security standards in a quantum era.

c. Collaboration with Industry: Governments collaborate with industry stakeholders, research institutions, and experts to develop quantum-resistant cryptographic standards and solutions.

d. National Security Considerations: National security agencies are closely monitoring the development of quantum computing and the potential threats it poses to critical infrastructure, including financial systems and cryptocurrencies.

2. Industry Initiatives:

a. Blockchain and Cryptocurrency Projects: Many blockchain and cryptocurrency projects are proactively researching and implementing quantum-resistant cryptographic algorithms to secure their networks.

b. Standards Development: Industry organizations, such as NIST (National Institute of Standards and Technology), are leading the development of post-quantum cryptographic standards. These standards provide guidance for implementing quantum-resistant security measures.

c. Education and Awareness: The cryptocurrency industry is educating users and stakeholders about the quantum threat and the importance of adopting quantum-resistant practices.

d. Collaboration with Quantum Experts: Cryptocurrency projects are collaborating with quantum experts and researchers to ensure the security and viability of quantum-resistant solutions.

e. Network Upgrades: Some cryptocurrency projects have introduced upgrades to transition to quantum-resistant algorithms, ensuring that their networks remain secure in a quantum computing environment.

f. ***Wallet and Infrastructure Security:*** Industry stakeholders, including wallet providers and infrastructure developers, are focusing on enhancing the security of private keys and endpoints against quantum attacks.

3. Research and Development:

a. ***Quantum-Resistant Cryptography:*** Cryptographers and researchers are actively developing quantum-resistant cryptographic algorithms that can be implemented in both government and industry contexts.

b. ***Simulation and Testing:*** Researchers are simulating and testing quantum attacks on cryptocurrency networks to understand their vulnerabilities and develop countermeasures.

c. ***Collaboration:*** Collaboration between academia, industry, and governments is fostering innovation and development in quantum-resistant cryptography.

4. Quantum Key Distribution (QKD):

a. ***Deployment in Critical Infrastructure:*** In some cases, QKD is being deployed in critical infrastructure to enhance the security of communications, including those related to cryptocurrencies and financial systems.

b. Research and Development: Ongoing research in QKD aims to make this technology more practical, cost-effective, and accessible for a broader range of applications.

In summary, both governments and the cryptocurrency industry are actively working to address the quantum threat by investing in research, developing standards, upgrading networks, and collaborating with experts. The goal is to ensure that digital assets and financial systems remain secure and resilient in the face of emerging quantum computing technology. Proactive measures and collaboration are crucial to prepare for the potential challenges posed by quantum computing.

Regulations and standards play a crucial role in promoting quantum-resistant security practices. They provide a framework for ensuring the security and integrity of digital systems and data, especially in a post-quantum era. Here's how regulations and standards contribute to the promotion of quantum-resistant security practices:

1. Setting Security Baselines:

Minimum Security Requirements: Regulations can establish minimum security requirements that organizations and systems must adhere to, including the use of quantum-resistant cryptographic algorithms. This ensures that security practices are consistent and robust across various sectors and industries.

Compliance Frameworks: Regulatory authorities can create compliance frameworks that organizations must follow to demonstrate that they have implemented quantum-resistant security measures effectively. This helps in the standardization of security practices.

2. Fostering Innovation and Research:

Research Funding: Governments can allocate funds for research into post-quantum cryptography and encourage the development of quantum-resistant cryptographic standards. These funds can be used to support research institutions and projects working on quantum-resistant solutions.

Collaboration: Regulatory bodies can encourage collaboration between researchers, industries, and government agencies to drive innovation in quantum-resistant security practices.

3. Encouraging Adoption:

Mandatory Adoption: Regulations can mandate the adoption of quantum-resistant cryptographic algorithms and security practices in critical infrastructure, financial systems, and other sectors. This ensures that organizations take the quantum threat seriously and implement necessary safeguards.

Incentives and Penalties: Regulatory bodies can provide incentives for organizations that proactively adopt quantum-resistant practices while imposing penalties for non-compliance. These measures encourage adherence to security standards.

4. Certification and Validation:

Certification Programs: Regulatory bodies can establish certification programs for quantum-resistant security practices. Organizations that meet these certification requirements can earn a seal of approval, demonstrating their commitment to security.

Third-Party Validation: Independent third-party organizations can validate that organizations are implementing quantum-resistant security measures effectively. This validation process provides an additional layer of assurance.

5. Collaboration and Standardization:

Industry Standards: Regulatory authorities can encourage the development of industry-wide standards for quantum-resistant security. These standards help ensure interoperability and consistency in security practices.

Partnerships: Regulators can foster partnerships between industry organizations, government agencies, and standards bodies to develop and promote quantum-resistant standards.

6. Public Awareness:

Education: Regulations can mandate that organizations provide education and training on quantum-resistant security practices to their employees and stakeholders. This helps raise awareness and understanding of the quantum threat.

7. Legal Frameworks:

Liability and Responsibility: Regulations can define liability and responsibility in the event of a security breach that results from a failure to adopt quantum-resistant practices. This legal framework encourages organizations to prioritize security.

Data Protection: Regulations related to data protection can require that personal and sensitive data be secured with quantum-resistant cryptography, ensuring the privacy of individuals.

In summary, regulations and standards are essential for promoting quantum-resistant security practices. They provide a structured and consistent approach to address the quantum threat, encourage innovation, and ensure that security measures are robust and effective. In a world where quantum computing poses new security challenges, regulatory and standardization efforts are key to maintaining the security and integrity of digital systems and data.

Several global initiatives and collaborations are underway to prepare for quantum-secure cryptocurrencies and to address the security challenges posed by quantum computing technology. These efforts involve governments, standards organizations, industry stakeholders, researchers, and experts in cryptography. Here are some notable initiatives and collaborations:

National Institute of Standards and Technology (NIST):

NIST is a U.S. federal agency that plays a leading role in standardizing cryptographic algorithms. NIST has been actively working on post-quantum cryptography and initiated the Post-Quantum Cryptography Standardization project. This project aims to develop and standardize quantum-resistant cryptographic algorithms.

European Telecommunications Standards Institute (ETSI):

ETSI is a European standards organization that has been working on quantum-safe standards for communication systems. Their Quantum-Safe Cryptography (QSC) Industry Specification Group focuses on ensuring the security of communication systems against quantum threats.

The Quantum Resistant Ledger (QRL):

The QRL is a blockchain project specifically designed to be quantum-resistant. It is working on developing a quantum-resistant ledger that uses cryptographic algorithms and methods believed to be secure against quantum attacks.

Quantum-Safe Crypto Project (QSCP):

QSCP is a consortium of academic institutions, research organizations, and industry stakeholders dedicated to advancing quantum-safe cryptography. They aim to develop and promote quantum-resistant cryptographic standards and solutions.

The Quantum-Safe Security Working Group (QSSWG):

The QSSWG, part of the Cloud Security Alliance, focuses on addressing the security challenges associated with quantum computing. It provides guidelines and best practices for securing cloud-based systems and networks in a post-quantum era.

International Collaboration:

Researchers, organizations, and governments from various countries collaborate on quantum-resistant research and standards development. International cooperation is vital to address the quantum threat comprehensively.

Research and Academic Collaborations:

Universities and research institutions worldwide are conducting research on post-quantum cryptography. Collaborations between academia and industry are key to developing and implementing quantum-resistant solutions.

Open-Source Initiatives:

Several open-source projects are focused on developing quantum-resistant cryptographic libraries and tools. These projects are accessible to developers and organizations looking to implement quantum-safe security measures.

Cryptocurrency Communities:

Many cryptocurrency communities are proactively researching and implementing quantum-resistant cryptographic algorithms and standards. They aim to safeguard their networks and digital assets against potential quantum threats.

Government Initiatives:

Some governments are investing in research and development related to quantum-resistant cryptography and blockchain technology. They recognize the importance of preparing for the quantum threat.

Private Sector Initiatives:

Private companies and financial institutions are investing in research and development to prepare for quantum-secure cryptocurrencies and to protect their financial systems and data.

These initiatives and collaborations reflect a growing awareness of the need to prepare for the quantum threat and the importance of securing digital assets and communication in a post-quantum era. By working together and pooling resources, global stakeholders are taking proactive steps to develop and implement quantum-resistant solutions for cryptocurrencies and beyond.

THE FUTURE OF CRYPTOCURRENCY SCURITY IN A QUANTUM WORLD:

The evolution of cryptocurrency security in the presence of quantum computing is a subject of intense speculation and research. While it's challenging to predict the future with certainty, we can make some educated speculations about how cryptocurrency security may evolve in a world with practical quantum computing:

1. ***Transition to Quantum-Resistant Cryptography:*** Cryptocurrency projects will increasingly adopt quantum-resistant cryptographic algorithms to protect transactions and digital assets. As quantum computing advances, the need for stronger encryption will become more apparent.

2. ***Early Adoption and Preparedness:*** Projects that are proactive in implementing quantum-resistant security measures will be better prepared for the quantum threat. Early adopters will likely have a competitive advantage in terms of security and trust.

3. ***Hard Forks and Network Upgrades:*** Many cryptocurrencies will undergo hard forks and network upgrades to transition to quantum-resistant standards.

These upgrades may cause temporary disruptions but are necessary for long-term security.

4. ***Quantum-Resistant Wallets:*** Quantum-resistant wallets will become essential for securing digital assets. Users will need to migrate their assets to quantum-safe wallets to ensure their private keys remain secure.

5. ***Increased Security Education:*** There will be a heightened focus on educating cryptocurrency users and stakeholders about the quantum threat and the steps they need to take to secure their assets.

6. ***Collaboration and Standards:*** The development of quantum-resistant standards and best practices will be crucial. Collaboration between industry, government, and research institutions will drive the adoption of these standards.

7. ***Regulations and Compliance:*** Regulatory bodies may introduce rules and regulations related to quantum-resistant security practices. Compliance with these regulations will become a priority for cryptocurrency projects.

8. ***Quantum Key Distribution (QKD):*** Quantum Key Distribution may find applications in securing cryptocurrency networks and communication channels,

providing an extra layer of security against quantum attacks.

9. ***Diversification of Consensus Mechanisms:*** Cryptocurrencies may diversify their consensus mechanisms to reduce their reliance on a single point of failure. Hybrid or multi-algorithm consensus models can provide additional security.

10. ***Blockchain Resilience:*** Cryptocurrencies will focus on improving their overall network resilience against quantum attacks, including the defense against potential 51% attacks by quantum miners.

11. ***Integration of Post-Quantum Cryptography:*** Post-quantum cryptographic techniques, such as lattice-based and code-based cryptography, will play a significant role in enhancing the security of cryptocurrency networks.

12. ***Quantum-Safe Testing and Simulations:*** Cryptocurrency projects will conduct regular testing and simulations to assess the network's vulnerability to quantum threats and to refine their quantum-resistant measures.

13. ***Innovation in Quantum Computing:*** Cryptocurrency projects may collaborate with quantum computing experts to better understand potential threats and to

develop countermeasures that stay ahead of developments in quantum computing technology.

14. *Consumer Demand for Quantum-Security:* As awareness of the quantum threat grows, users may favor cryptocurrencies and platforms that prioritize quantum-resistant security measures, leading to increased demand for such solutions.

15. *Ongoing Research:* Cryptographic research will remain a dynamic field, adapting to emerging quantum threats and exploring new security solutions.

In the presence of quantum computing, the evolution of cryptocurrency security will require adaptation, collaboration, and a proactive approach to protect digital assets and transactions from emerging threats. While quantum computing presents challenges, it also opens the door to new security innovations and practices.

The development of quantum-resistant cryptography and security measures is an active area of research and innovation. Here are some potential advancements in this field:

1. *Lattice-Based Cryptography:* Lattice-based cryptography is a promising area of research. Advances in lattice-based cryptographic algorithms can lead to

stronger security against quantum attacks. Researchers are working on optimizing lattice-based schemes for practical implementation.

2. ***Code-Based Cryptography:*** Code-based cryptography, which relies on error-correcting codes, remains a strong candidate for post-quantum security. Ongoing research aims to improve the efficiency and performance of code-based schemes.

3. ***Multivariate Quadratic Equations (MQ):*** MQ cryptography is another approach being explored. Advancements in MQ-based schemes can lead to practical, quantum-resistant solutions.

4. ***Hash-Based Signatures:*** Hash-based cryptographic signatures are considered highly secure against quantum attacks. Research is focused on making these schemes more efficient and suitable for various applications, including digital currencies.

5. ***Supersingular Isogeny Diffie-Hellman (SIDH):*** SIDH is an area of active research in the context of quantum-resistant cryptography. Further advances may lead to more efficient and practical implementations.

6. ***Quantum-Safe Key Exchange Protocols:*** Researchers are working on quantum-resistant key exchange

protocols that can be used to secure communications and transactions in a post-quantum world.

7. ***Quantum Key Distribution (QKD):*** QKD technology is continually advancing, making it more practical and cost-effective. Widespread adoption of QKD can enhance the security of communication channels for digital currencies.

8. ***Post-Quantum Secure Hash Functions:*** Research into developing post-quantum secure hash functions is crucial. These functions are used in various aspects of blockchain and cryptocurrency technology.

9. ***Quantum-Resistant Smart Contracts:*** Smart contract platforms are exploring quantum-resistant programming languages and frameworks to ensure the security and functionality of smart contracts in the presence of quantum threats.

10. ***Quantum-Safe Wallets:*** The development of quantum-resistant wallets is essential to secure private keys and digital assets against quantum attacks.

11. ***Integration with Existing Systems:*** Advancements in quantum-resistant cryptography will focus on ensuring compatibility with existing systems, making the transition to quantum-safe solutions more seamless.

12. *Security Audits and Testing:* Comprehensive security audits and testing of quantum-resistant solutions will help identify and address vulnerabilities and ensure their robustness.

13. *User Education and Awareness:* Efforts will continue to educate users, developers, and organizations about the importance of quantum-resistant security practices and the steps required to protect digital assets.

14. *Quantum Computing Simulations:* Simulating quantum attacks and vulnerabilities will enable researchers to understand and develop countermeasures against potential quantum threats.

15. *Government and Industry Collaboration:* Collaborative efforts between governments, industry stakeholders, and research institutions will drive the development and adoption of quantum-resistant standards and solutions.

16. *Standardization and Certification:* The establishment of global standards and certification programs for quantum-resistant cryptography will provide a framework for ensuring security.

Advancements in quantum-resistant cryptography and security measures are essential to prepare for the quantum threat. As quantum computing technology progresses, the field of post-quantum cryptography will continue to evolve to provide robust and practical solutions for securing digital assets and communication.